UNDERSTANDING
MODERN
ISRAEL

Published by
Lion Hudson Limited
Prama House,
267 Banbury Road, Summertown,
Oxford, OX2 7HT
www.lionhudson.com

ISBN 978 0 85721 998 5
e-ISBN 978 1 80030 014 9
First edition 2021

Acknowledgments
Unless otherwise indicated, all Scripture quotations are taken from the *Holy
Bible*, New Living Translation, copyright © 1996, 2004, 2015 by Tyndale House
Foundation: Anglicized Text Version © SPCK 2018. Used by permission of
Tyndale House Publishers, Inc., Carol Stream, Illinois 60188, USA, and SPCK,
London, UK. All rights reserved.

Scripture quotations marked NIV taken from the Holy Bible, New International
Version Anglicised. Copyright © 1979, 1984, 2011 Biblica, formerly
International Bible Society. Used by permission of Hodder & Stoughton Ltd, an
Hachette UK company. All rights reserved. "NIV" is a registered trademark of
Biblica. UK trademark number 1448790.

A catalogue record for this book is available from the British Library

Printed and bound in the UK, May 2021, LH26

UNDERSTANDING
MODERN
ISRAEL
A Biblical Perspective

JULIA FISHER

MONARCH

I would like to dedicate this book to Ann Pawson, a true friend and fellow traveller on this journey to understand modern Israel and all that God is doing there. Thank you Ann.

CONTENTS

INTRODUCTION

The story of Israel is supernatural because never has a nation been exiled from its land only to return sometime later and re-establish itself as an independent state. In Israel's case, this has happened not once, but three times. The question is, why?

And, you may be wondering, why should I care? What has it got to do with me?

This is a book of stories – the story of Israel and the Jewish people and, more recently, stories of people living in Israel and the West Bank today who are believers in Jesus. Why is that remarkable, you ask? Because until approximately seventy years ago, there had not been a recognizable group of Jewish believers in Israel since the early church came into being after the death and resurrection of Jesus. Those events are well documented in the book of Acts and make exciting reading!

But then, just as the early church was growing in number and getting established, in AD 70 the Romans sacked Jerusalem, the people fled or were killed, and life there came to an abrupt halt.

However, we live in extraordinary times! Over the past one hundred years, and particularly during the past forty years, something has changed. Today not only are there several thousand Jewish believers in Israel, but there are also many Israeli Arab Christians and Palestinian Christians, some of whom are former Muslims – all sharing the same land!

For the past twenty years, I've been following and reporting on this story. It is a story that has emerged slowly but surely and, for Christians, surely requires our understanding.

Modern Israel has risen out of the horror and ashes of the Holocaust – that dark time in history when, during the Second World War, European Jewry was hunted and killed by the Nazis whose avowed intent was to rid the world of Jewish people. However, they didn't succeed and, in 1948, against all the odds, Israel became a nation once again.

But how are we, as Christians who believe the Bible, meant to understand modern Israel? From a distance it appears a divided, unjust place where the two people groups who share the land are constantly fighting. While writing this book during January 2020, Donald Trump, President of the United States of America, announced his peace plan for Israelis and Palestinians. But can there be a lasting peace based on a political solution? There are many schools of thought on this and doubtless the arguments will continue. It is interesting to note, however, that to date, a political solution for this troubled land has not been found. So let us return to the question: how are we, as Christians who believe the Bible, meant to understand modern Israel?

In this book, we will attempt to look at the story of Israel from God's perspective. When we look at the story of Israel from a biblical perspective, this takes us above the level of politics and opinion to another realm altogether. It takes us to the Bible where we find the history of Israel told in great detail and the future of Israel and her people explained too.

One of the challenges we face today is sifting through the many differing, strongly felt opinions we hear through our news channels and other media. The danger here is that we can easily be influenced and thus the understanding we have becomes skewed by the opinions of others.

This is a book of stories stretching back 4,000 years and comes right up to date with true life stories that are emerging today. Then we will take a glance into the future and, by the end, I hope you will have engaged with this story – because it is a story that involves every one of us.

1

THE FIRST EXILE IN EGYPT

To understand modern Israel from a biblical perspective, we have to start at the beginning with the question, "Who are the Jewish people and why have they been exiled from the land of Israel three times?" When did it all begin?

The story of modern Israel began way back in history, approximately 4,000 years ago, in 2000 BC, and it is well documented.[1] What's more, each of the three exiles was predicted – accurately foretold. How do we know this?

Remember the story of Joseph and his multicoloured coat? Joseph was the favourite son of his father, Jacob. His grandfather was Isaac, whose father was Abraham, who became the founding father of the people of Israel when he left his homeland of Ur of the Chaldeans (in modern-day Iraq) in around 2000 BC, as mentioned in Genesis:

> *The Lord had said to Abram, "Leave your native country, your relatives, and your father's family, and go to the land that I will show you. I will make you into a great nation. I will bless you and make you famous, and you will be a blessing to others. I will bless those who bless you and curse those who treat you with contempt. All the families on earth will be blessed through you."*
>
> GENESIS 12:1–3

---

1   Even secular historians acknowledge the validity of the Old Testament as a historical, archaeological source.

Abraham married Sarah but they were unable to have children. This caused Abraham some grief because God had promised that he would become the father of a great nation!

He remonstrated with God,

> *"O Sovereign Lord, what good are all your blessings when I don't even have a son?"*
> GENESIS 15:2

In Abraham's mind, his servant, Eliezer of Damascus, would inherit all his wealth and become his heir. But the Lord reassured Abraham that he would, in time, have a son of his own who would be his rightful heir. The Lord also told Abraham that years later:

> *"You can be sure that your descendants will be strangers in a foreign land, where they will be oppressed as slaves for 400 years. But I will punish the nation that enslaves them, and in the end they will come away with great wealth... After four generations your descendants will return here to this land."*
> GENESIS 15:13–16

It would be some time before Abraham and Sarah had the son that God had promised. Meanwhile, they took matters into their own hands. In doubt and despair that Sarah would ever conceive and have a child of her own, Sarah gave Abraham her Egyptian servant Hagar as a second wife and Ishmael was born. Abraham was eighty-six years old at that time and no doubt delighted to have a son at last; but Ishmael was not the son God had promised.

Time passed and if ever things looked impossible, thirteen years later, when Abraham was ninety-nine years old, the Lord appeared to him again:

"Sarah, your wife, will give birth to a son for you. You will name him Isaac, and I will confirm my covenant with him and his descendants as an everlasting covenant. As for Ishmael, I will bless him also, just as you have asked. I will make him extremely fruitful and multiply his descendants. He will become the father of twelve princes and I will make him a great nation. But my covenant will be confirmed with Isaac, who will be born to you and Sarah about this time next year."

GENESIS 17:19–21

And it happened! A year later Isaac was born. He later married Rebekah and they had twin sons, Esau and Jacob. Although Esau was theoretically the elder as he had been born first, the story of his carefree life and lack of respect for his parents in marrying foreign women with pagan religions resulted in Jacob easily tricking him out of his birthright and becoming his father's heir.

Jacob had twelve sons, his favourite being Joseph (aka "the dreamer"). This special status – combined with Joseph's arrogance – caused his brothers to loathe him. One day, when they were miles away from home minding their father's sheep, their opportunity came to get rid of Joseph. Joseph arrived, wearing his coat of many colours, bringing some food from their father who had sent him to find out how his brothers were faring. At the same time, some Ishmaelite traders passed by en route to Egypt. The brothers seized the opportunity – rather than kill Joseph, they would sell him to these traders who were happy to buy a strong, healthy young man they could sell as a slave when they reached Egypt. Bound by ropes, Joseph was powerless to resist. We can only imagine what he must have been thinking. Would he ever see his father again? And what about those dreams? Had they been a figment of his imagination?

Arriving in Egypt, Joseph was bought by Potiphar, one of Pharaoh's personal staff. For a while, all went relatively well for Joseph – Potiphar entrusted him not only with running his entire household, but also with his business dealings. We read,

Potiphar gave Joseph complete administrative responsibility over everything he owned. With Joseph there, he didn't worry about a thing – except what kind of food to eat!
GENESIS 39:6

The story of how Joseph eventually became Pharaoh's right-hand man is painful in the extreme. Joseph was a handsome young man. Potiphar's wife was lonely with too much time on her hands and she tried to seduce Joseph. He resisted: she became angry and lied that he had tried to rape her. Potiphar was understandably upset that Joseph, having been trusted with everything Potiphar owned, should then betray him in this way. He threw Joseph into the prison that also held the king's prisoners.

But, as we read, God was with Joseph. His gift at being able to interpret dreams brought about his release from prison when Pharaoh had two dreams that caused him great distress. His own magicians and wise men were unable to explain what the dreams meant, but the king's cup-bearer, who had shared the same prison cell as Joseph for a time, remembered how Joseph had once interpreted one of his dreams. After a shave and a change of clothes, Joseph was hastily brought before Pharaoh. Pharaoh was so impressed by Joseph for explaining his dreams warning of impending famine that he put him in charge of ensuring enough food was stored during the seven years of plentiful harvests, before the predicted seven years of famine.

Jacob, meanwhile, had long given up hope of ever seeing his favourite son again. His brothers had returned home after selling Joseph into slavery and taken his coat of many colours back to their father. They had daubed the coat in the blood of a slaughtered animal to make it look as though Joseph had been killed by a wild animal. But, a few years later, when famine hit the land of Israel, Jacob sent ten of his sons down to Egypt to buy grain – but Benjamin, the youngest, remained at home with his father. Joseph recognized them immediately. They, however, did not recognize him. The dream of bowing down before their younger brother had come true without them realizing it.

Jacob was eventually reunited with Joseph. Pharaoh generously insisted that the entire family – wives, children, servants, and livestock – moved to live in Goshen which was a fertile area of Egypt well suited to their lifestyle of keeping large herds of sheep and goats while living apart from the Egyptian people (who despised shepherds). This was the start of the story of the Children of Israel becoming a nation. However, 400 years later, they would be driven out of Egypt and return to the Promised Land, just as had been foretold. Jacob arrived in Egypt with seventy family members. When the Israelites left Egypt 400 years later, their numbers had increased to 600,000 men plus women and children (Exodus 12:37). They had become a nation!

But a nation living in a foreign land would not be able to stay there for ever. The time would come when they had to return to their own land.

Who would lead them out of Egypt?

After their initial warm welcome by the Pharaoh of Joseph's day, the Pharaoh of 400 years later was less kindly disposed to the Israelites.

In time, Joseph and all of his brothers died, ending that entire generation. But their descendants, the Israelites, had many children and grandchildren. In fact, they multiplied so greatly that they became extremely powerful and filled the land.

Eventually, a new king came to power in Egypt who knew nothing about Joseph or what he had done. He said to his people, "Look, the people of Israel now outnumber us and are stronger than we are. We must make a plan to keep them from growing even more. If we don't, and if war breaks out, they will join our enemies and fight against us. Then they will escape from the country.

So the Egyptians made the Israelites their slaves. They appointed brutal slave drivers over them, hoping to wear them down with crushing labour. They forced them to build the cities of Pithom and Rameses as supply centres for the king. But the more the Egyptians oppressed them, the more the Israelites multiplied and spread, and the more alarmed the Egyptians became. So the Egyptians worked the people of Israel without mercy. They made their lives bitter, forcing them to mix mortar and make bricks and do all the work in the fields. They were ruthless in all their demands.

Then Pharaoh, the king of Egypt, gave this order to the Hebrew midwives, Shiphrah and Puah: "When you help the Hebrew women as they give birth, watch as they deliver. If the baby is a boy, kill him; if it is a girl, let her live." But because the midwives feared God, they refused to obey the king's order. They allowed the boys to live, too.

So the king of Egypt called for the midwives. "Why have you done this?" he demanded. "Why have you allowed the boys to live?"

"The Hebrew women are not like the Egyptian women," the midwives replied. "They are more vigorous and have their babies so quickly that we cannot get there in time!"

So God was good to the midwives, and the Israelites continued to multiply, growing more and more powerful. And because the midwives feared God, he gave them families of their own.

Then Pharaoh gave this order to all his people: "Throw every newborn Hebrew boy into the Nile River. But you may let the girls live."
EXODUS 1:6–22

The birth of Moses – 1500 BC

Moses could not have been born at a more dangerous time. Thanks to the courage of his mother, combined with the ingenuity of his sister, Moses survived. Rather than being drowned in the River Nile, his life was saved when he was rescued, and later adopted by, an Egyptian princess. He received an Egyptian education and became familiar with court life. Having been raised by his own mother for the first few years of his life, he was well aware of his Hebrew roots. He watched as his own people were suffering under harsh slavery; brutally treated by their Egyptian masters. One day he took matters into his own hands and murdered one of the slave masters for being viciously cruel to a Hebrew man. However, he had been seen and was shocked and terrified to discover he had been found out.

> *Then Moses was afraid, thinking "Everyone knows what I did." And sure enough, Pharaoh heard what had happened, and he tried to kill Moses. But Moses fled from Pharaoh and went to live in the land of Midian.*
> EXODUS 2:14–16

Moses stayed in Midian for forty years. He settled there, married and had children. At the same time, the misery of his own people back in Egypt worsened to the point where they were struggling to survive under the callous treatment being meted out to them.

> *They cried out for help, and their cry rose up to God. God heard their groaning, and he remembered his covenant promise to Abraham, Isaac, and Jacob. He looked down on the people of Israel and knew it was time to act.*
> EXODUS 2:23–25

Exodus from Egypt – the first return from exile

The Israelites had lived in Egypt for 400 years; it was time to leave.

The process of preparing the Israelites to leave Egypt involved persuading Moses to become their leader and then persuading Pharaoh to let them go. Both were reluctant! Eventually Moses agreed that, with the help of his brother Aaron, he would take on the task. But Pharaoh became so stubborn that not even the dreadful plagues persuaded him to allow the Children of Israel to leave. It was only when the firstborn sons and firstborn male animals of every Egyptian family died on the night of the Passover that he eventually drove them out.

What was or is the Passover?

To understand the meaning of the Passover we have to understand what happened on the night the Israelites left Egypt. God had given Moses instructions on how to prepare the people to leave:

Announce to the whole community of Israel that on the tenth day of this month each family must choose a lamb or a young goat for a sacrifice, one animal for each household. If a family is too small to eat a whole animal, let them share with another family in the neighbourhood. Divide the animal according to the size of each family and how much they can eat. The animal you select must be a one-year-old male, either a sheep or a goat, with no defects.

Take special care of this chosen animal until the evening of the fourteenth day of this first month. Then the whole assembly of the community of Israel must slaughter their lamb or young goat at twilight. They are to take some of the blood and smear it on the sides and top of the doorframes of the houses where they eat the animal. That same night they must roast the meat over a fire and eat it along with bitter salad greens and bread made without yeast... Be fully dressed, wear your sandals, and carry your walking stick in your hand. Eat the food with urgency, for this is the Lord's Passover. On that night I will pass through the land of Egypt and strike down every firstborn son and firstborn male animal in the land of Egypt. I will execute judgement against all the gods of Egypt, for I am the Lord! But the blood on your doorposts will serve as a sign, marking the houses where you are staying. When I see the blood, I will pass over you. This plague of death will not touch you when I strike the land of Egypt.

This is a day to remember. Each year, from generation to generation, you must celebrate it as a special festival to the Lord.

EXODUS 12:3–14

That night the people of Israel left Rameses and started for Succoth. There were about 600,000 men, plus all the women and children. And they were all travelling on foot.

EXODUS 12:37, AUTHOR'S TRANSLATION

Since then, the Passover has been celebrated by Jewish people every year in the spring as a vivid reminder of the time God miraculously brought the Israelites safely out of Egypt. And for the past 2,000 years, Christians and Jewish believers in Jesus understand the Passover is a picture of the sacrifice of Jesus' death on the cross. The Israelites were told to sprinkle the blood of the lambs on their doorposts so that the angel of death would pass over their homes on the night when the firstborn in Egypt died. In the same way, believers in Jesus understand that they are saved from eternal death and separation from God – they believe that Jesus died in their place and that, through the shedding of his blood, they are saved and will spend eternity with him.

Why did God bring the Israelites out of Egypt to live in Israel?

We have seen how it all started with one man – Abraham – and God's promise that he would become the father of a great nation and all the families of the earth would be blessed through him.

We have seen how Abraham believed God. Yes, he made mistakes but, nevertheless, he obeyed God – and from one man came a family, and from that family grew a nation. Then it was time for the next part of God's plan to come to pass. The nation had to understand its unique identity and move back to its own land in order to discover its destiny. The Exodus was the beginning of God shaping and teaching a nation that would come to know him as the one and only true God.

You have been set apart as holy to the Lord your God, and he has chosen you from all the nations of the earth to be his own special treasure.
DEUTERONOMY 14:2

During the forty years in the wilderness the people witnessed how God was with them, looking after them and encouraging them every step of the way. He made a path for them through the Red Sea. He dealt with the Egyptian army that was chasing them. He was there in the pillar of fire at night, and in the cloud that led them during the day. They were fed daily with manna. Their clothes did not wear out. He gave them his laws. After Moses died and Joshua became their leader, God told them how to enter and conquer the land that he had promised them. Always the proviso was to obey the Lord.

Would they heed this advice and remain true, or would they turn away from the God of Abraham, Isaac, and Jacob and follow other gods?

The answer to that question was given to Moses just before he died and the Children of Israel entered the Promised Land.

The Lord said to Moses, "You are about to die and join your ancestors. After you are gone, these people will begin to worship foreign gods, the gods of the land where they are going. They will abandon me and break my covenant that I have made with them. Then my anger will blaze forth against them. I will abandon them, hiding my face from them, and they will be devoured. Terrible trouble will come down on them, and on that day they will say, 'These disasters have come down on us because God is no longer among us!' At that time I will hide my face from them on account of all the evil they commit by worshipping other gods."

DEUTERONOMY 31:16-18

They were warned about the consequences of disobedience many times and sadly, as we will now explore, it was because of disobedience and a turning away from God that the people of Israel would find themselves, in 605 BC, once more going in to exile – this time, taken as captives to Babylon.

2

THE SECOND EXILE
IN BABYLON

The story of the Old Testament is the story of God's dealings with Israel and Israel's attitude to God. For almost a thousand years, from 1500 BC to 600 BC, we read how Israel had judges and then kings to lead her. Some of these judges and kings honoured and respected the God of Israel, such as King David and his son Solomon (who later built the first Temple in Jerusalem, around tenth-century BC), but others displeased God with their refusal to believe in him.

It was during the reign of King Manasseh – who did not honour or respect the God of Israel – that Israel's depravity reached an all-time low.

Manasseh was twelve years old when he became king [circa 697 BC], and he reigned in Jerusalem fifty-five years… He did what was evil in the Lord's sight, following the detestable practices of the pagan nations that the Lord had driven from the land ahead of the Israelites. He rebuilt the pagan shrines his father, Hezekiah, had destroyed. He constructed altars for Baal and set up an Asherah pole, just as King Ahab of Israel had done. He also bowed before all the powers of the heavens and worshipped them.

He built pagan altars in the Temple of the Lord, the place where the Lord had said, "My name will remain in Jerusalem forever." … Manasseh also sacrificed his own son in the fire. He practised sorcery and divination, and he consulted with mediums and psychics. He did much that was evil in the Lord's sight, arousing his anger.

Manasseh even made a carved image of Asherah and set it up in the Temple, the very place where the Lord had told David and his son Solomon: "My name will be honoured forever in this Temple and in Jerusalem – the city I have chosen from among all the other tribes of Israel. If the Israelites will be careful to obey my commands – all the laws my servant Moses gave them – I will not send them into exile from this land that I gave their ancestors." But the people refused to listen, and Manasseh led them to do even more evil than the pagan nations that the Lord had destroyed when the people of Israel entered the land.

Then the Lord said through his servants the prophets: "King Manasseh of Judah has done many detestable things. He is even more wicked than the Amorites, who lived in this land before Israel. … So this is what the Lord, the God of Israel, says: I will bring such disaster on Jerusalem and Judah that the ears of those who hear about it will tingle with horror… I will wipe away the people of Jerusalem as one wipes a dish and turns it upside down. Then I will reject even the remnant of my own people who are left, and I will hand them over as plunder for their enemies. For they have done great evil in my sight and have angered me ever since their ancestors came out of Egypt."

2 KINGS 21:1–15

The three stages of the second exile

As predicted, just a few years later, the second exile began. There were three stages: the first was in 605 BC, during King Jehoiakim's reign, when King Nebuchadnezzar of Babylon invaded the land of Judah, besieged Jerusalem, and returned to Babylon taking with him some of the sacred objects from the Temple of God. He placed them in the treasure house of his god in the land of Babylonia. He also took with him some of the young men from Judah's royal family, including Daniel, Hananiah, Mishael, and Azariah.

A few years later, in 597 BC, Nebuchadnezzar returned to Jerusalem with a large army and besieged the city. The next king, King Jehoiachin, was taken prisoner and we read:

Nebuchadnezzar carried away all the treasures from the Lord's Temple and the royal palace. He stripped away all the gold objects that King Solomon of Israel had placed in the Temple. King Nebuchadnezzar took all of Jerusalem captive, including all the commanders and the best of the soldiers, craftsmen, and artisans – 10,000 in all. Only the poorest people were left in the land.

2 KINGS 24:13–14

Finally, in 586 BC, Nebuchadnezzar returned to crush King Zedekiah and the remaining people in Jerusalem – and we read that, this time, he led his entire army against Jerusalem.

They surrounded the city and built siege ramps against its walls. Jerusalem was kept under siege until the eleventh year of King Zedekiah's reign. ... The famine in the city had become very severe, and the last of the food was entirely gone. Then a section of the city wall was broken down. Since the city was surrounded by the Babylonians, the soldiers waited for nightfall and escaped through the gate between the two walls behind the king's garden. Then they headed toward the Jordan Valley.

But the Babylonian troops chased the king and overtook him on the plains of Jericho, for his men had all deserted him and scattered. ... Nebuzaradan, the captain of the guard and an official of the Babylonian king, arrived in Jerusalem.

He burned down the Temple of the Lord, the royal palace, and all the houses of Jerusalem. He destroyed all the important buildings in the city. Then he supervised the entire Babylonian army as they tore down the walls of Jerusalem on every side. Then Nebuzaradan, the captain of the guard, took as exiles the rest of the people who remained in the city. … But the captain of the guard allowed some of the poorest people to stay behind to care for the vineyards and fields.

2 KINGS 25:1-12

The destruction of Jerusalem was complete

The magnificent Temple that Solomon had built was destroyed and all the Temple treasures were carried away to Babylon. Jerusalem lay in ruins. Apart from a remnant of the poorest Jewish people, the entire population was taken captive to Babylon where they were to remain for seventy years. How do we know this?

As already mentioned, everything that happened to the Jewish people had been foretold. In this case, it was the prophet Jeremiah who not only warned the people of the impending disaster that was about to befall them (but which they refused to listen to), but who also prophesied:

"You will be in Babylon for seventy years. But then I will come and do for you all the good things I have promised, and I will bring you home again. For I know the plans I have for you," says the Lord. "They are plans for good and not for disaster, to give you a future and a hope. In those days when you pray, I will listen. If you look for me wholeheartedly, you will find me. I will be found by you," says the Lord. "I will end your captivity and restore your fortunes. I will gather you out of the nations where I sent you and will bring you home again to your own land."

JEREMIAH 29:10-14

Return from the second exile

And it happened just as the Lord had prophesied through Jeremiah – seventy years after the Jewish exiles first arrived in Babylon, the power of the mighty Babylonians was broken when, in 539 BC, they were overthrown by the Persian king, Cyrus. A year later, in 538 BC, Cyrus issued a decree and sent it throughout his kingdom.

This is what King Cyrus of Persia says: "The Lord, the God of heaven, has given me all the kingdoms of the earth. He has appointed me to build him a Temple at Jerusalem, which is in Judah. Any of you who are his people may go to Jerusalem in Judah to rebuild this Temple of the Lord, the God of Israel, who lives in Jerusalem. And may your God be with you! Wherever this Jewish remnant is found, let their neighbours contribute toward their expenses by giving them silver and gold, supplies for the journey, and livestock, as well as a voluntary offering for the Temple of God in Jerusalem."

EZRA 1:2–4

How did Cyrus know that God had chosen him to rebuild the Temple in Jerusalem? Could it be that he was aware of Isaiah's prophecy written 200 years earlier?

When I say of Cyrus, "He is my shepherd," he will certainly do as I say. He will command, "Rebuild Jerusalem"; he will say, "Restore the Temple".

ISAIAH 44:28

We will never know how Cyrus was stirred to take this action. But we do know that this was the signal for the return of the exiles to Jerusalem – and included in the first group of exiles to return to the land was Zerubbabel. His grandfather was Jehoiachin, one of the kings of Jerusalem who was taken into

25

captivity under King Nebuchadnezzar of Babylon. Zerubbabel was also a descendant of King David and therefore in direct line of the ancestry of Jesus.

The story of how the second Temple came to be rebuilt and the eventual return of the exiles is well documented in the books of Ezra and Nehemiah. The foundation was laid but then work came to a halt for seventeen years because of local opposition by non-Jews:

> *Then the local residents tried to discourage and frighten the people of Judah to keep them from their work. They bribed agents to work against them and to frustrate their aims. This went on during the entire reign of King Cyrus of Persia and lasted until King Darius of Persia took the throne.*
> EZRA 4:4–5

However, by 515 BC the work was finished and

> *The Temple of God was then dedicated with great joy by the people of Israel, the priests, the Levites, and the rest of the people who had returned from exile.*
> EZRA 6:16

Did all the Jewish exiles accept King Cyrus' offer allowing them to leave Babylon and return to Jerusalem? The answer to that question is "no". Approximately 50,000 Jewish exiles chose to return – out of an estimated population of between 2 and 3 million people. Many chose to stay. Centuries later, a Jewish community still existed in what is now Iraq. They had undoubtedly settled and built a comfortable life for themselves. When they had left, Jerusalem was in ruins and it required rebuilding. The thought of returning 900 miles to the city on foot was less appealing than staying in Babylon.

The effect of the exile

What effect did the exile have on the Jewish people returning to live in Israel? After the hard work of rebuilding the Temple was completed, Ezra, the priest, led the people in a solemn act of repentance and rededication. Temple worship was restored. Priests and Levites resumed their duties. The Law of Moses was read to the people with startling effect.

In October, when the Israelites had settled in their towns, all the people assembled with a unified purpose at the square just inside the Water Gate. They asked Ezra the scribe to bring out the Book of the Law of Moses, which the Lord had given for Israel to obey.

So on October 8 Ezra the priest brought the Book of the Law before the assembly, which included the men and women and all the children old enough to understand. He faced the square just inside the Water Gate from early morning until noon and read aloud to everyone who could understand. All the people listened closely to the Book of the Law.

Ezra the scribe stood on a high wooden platform that had been made for the occasion ... in full view of all the people. When they saw him open the book, they all rose to their feet.
NEHEMIAH 8:1–5

This was the start of a spiritual reawakening in Israel and we read later in chapter 9:1-3:

On October 31 the people assembled again, and this time they fasted and dressed in sackcloth and sprinkled dust on their heads. Those of Israelite descent separated themselves from all foreigners as they confessed their own sins and the sins of their ancestors. They remained standing in place for three hours while the Book of the Law of the Lord their God

27

was read aloud to them. Then for three more hours they confessed their sins and worshipped the Lord their God.

The leaders of the Levites then reminded the people of their history, the call of Abraham and the covenant that God had made with him, of the exodus from Egypt, and the forty years wandering in the desert as a result of rebelling against God.

You… brought them into the land you had promised to their ancestors.

They went in and took possession of the land. You subdued whole nations before them…

But despite all this, they were disobedient and rebelled against you. They turned their backs on your Law, they killed the prophets who warned them to return to you, and they committed terrible blasphemies. So you handed them over to their enemies, who made them suffer. But in their time of trouble they cried to you, and you heard them from heaven. In your great mercy, you sent them liberators who rescued them from their enemies.

NEHEMIAH 9:23-24, 26-27

At the end of this meeting, we read in Nehemiah 10 about how the people renewed their covenant with the Lord to obey the laws of Moses. They promised together not to neglect the Temple of God. But for how much longer?

We will now consider the circumstances that led to the third exile of the Jewish people from the land of Israel in AD 70, after the death and resurrection of Jesus. Where did they go and where are they now? And that will bring us to the present day!

3

THE THIRD
AND LONGEST EXILE

We have learned that the Second Temple was completed in 515 BC and Temple worship was restored. But as history tells us, in AD 70 on the ninth of Av in the Hebrew calendar (the same day as the destruction of the first Temple in 586 BC), the Roman army destroyed this Temple and it was burned to the ground. Thousands of Jews were slaughtered. Others were sold into slavery while others fled and sought refuge in other nations. Apart from a small remnant, Jerusalem was emptied of people and lay in ruins once again – this time for 1,900 years. We now have to ask what caused this disaster.

What happened between 515 BC – AD 70?

This period of over 400 years is often referred to as the "Silent Years" – years when the Jewish people (who had returned from exile in Babylon and rebuilt the Temple) started the process of rebuilding their lives and re-establishing themselves as a nation in their homeland of Israel.

The 400 years of silence are also known as the years when God did not speak to the people in Israel. The last words he spoke came through the prophet Malachi:

"Look, I am sending you the prophet Elijah before the great and dreadful day of the Lord arrives. His preaching will

turn the hearts of fathers to their children, and the hearts of children to their fathers. Otherwise I will come and strike the land with a curse."

MALACHI 4:5-6

The next words he spoke came through John the Baptist who prepared the people for the coming of the Messiah.

As we will now discover, during this 400 year period, the Jews were not able to get on with their lives or run their nation alone. There was plenty of outside interference! After the Persians, the Greeks conquered Israel. They were led by Alexander the Great and it was under his influence that Greek became the lingua franca, the most commonly spoken language of the day. After Alexander's untimely death at the age of thirty-two, his extensive empire divided between his four generals – Ptolemy, Seleucus, Cassander, and Antigonus. The Ptolemies who were based in Egypt ruled Israel for a time and the Jews were left in relative peace. However, when the Seleucids came to power, they were cruel and forced the Jews into pagan practices and set up altars to pagan gods in the temple courts. Many Jews rebelled against the Seleucids; this became known as the Maccabean revolt. Eventually, the Jews won their independence but that only lasted until 63 BC when the Romans conquered the land. In 37 BC, Herod the Great was made "King of the Jews".

Was he called Herod the Great because of his ambitious building projects? It was this Herod who enlarged the Temple platform and restored the Temple to become the impressive building that was there in Jesus' time. Herod was ambitious and keen to be seen as being successful in the eyes of Rome. However, he was cruel and had a jealous and suspicious nature. When he met the wise men and heard about the birth of Jesus, the "King of the Jews" they had come to worship in Bethlehem, he ordered the massacre of all the baby boys there. He was not going to allow anybody to usurp his position.

Israel in the time of Jesus

The Gospel writers tell us much about the Roman occupation of the land of Israel and the people's cry for freedom from these cruel oppressors. Many saw Jesus as being the one who would bring about this freedom. However, Jesus fastidiously side-stepped the politics of the day and concentrated instead on preaching about the kingdom of God. He came to bring deliverance of the captives in a different way – his was a message of repentance and turning to God.

The problem was that the people – and especially the religious leaders of the day – did not believe him.

The tragedy of AD 70

Why did the tragedy of AD 70 occur? The answer to this question can be clearly understood from the words of Jesus spoken in the final days before his death:

But as he came closer to Jerusalem and saw the city ahead, he began to weep. "How I wish today that you of all people would understand the way to peace. But now it is too late, and peace is hidden from your eyes. Before long your enemies will build ramparts against your walls and encircle you and close in on you from every side. They will crush you into the ground, and your children with you. Your enemies will not leave a single stone in place, because you did not recognize it when God visited you."

LUKE 19:41–44

"Because you did not recognize it when God visited you." The religious leaders had rejected Jesus and refused to believe he was the promised Messiah. Jesus was warning his disciples that, very soon, the Roman army would build ramparts against the walls of Jerusalem and destroy the city. No wonder he began to weep – Jesus could see what would soon happen. He knew thousands would be killed and others would flee for their lives. The land would be empty again, this time for a very long period of time.

We go on to read in Luke's Gospel how Jesus then "entered the Temple and began to drive out the people selling animals for sacrifices" – such was his indignation at the way they were turning the very place where God was to be worshipped into "a den of thieves" (Luke 19:45–46).

We can only imagine what his disciples made of the highly charged atmosphere that would have resulted from such a physical confrontation. At the same time, Jesus was being verbally challenged at every turn by the teachers of religious law, the Sadducees, the Pharisees and the leading priests, all of whom were trying to trick him into saying something that would give them the opportunity they so desperately wanted to have him arrested. They hated him.

It would appear that the disciples had not yet fully understood that Jesus would not be with them for much longer. They still saw him as invincible, the one who would usher in a new order. They could not comprehend that he was going to die. Imagine their shock when they innocently started chatting among themselves while admiring the magnificence of the Temple:

Some of his disciples began talking about the majestic stonework of the Temple and the memorial decorations on the walls. But Jesus said, "The time is coming when all these things will be completely demolished. Not one stone will be left on top of another!"

"Teacher," they asked, "when will all this happen? What sign will show us that these things are about to take place?"
LUKE 21:5–7

Hindsight is a wonderful thing. We know what happened next. But for those disciples, the thought of anybody being able to destroy the Temple was incomprehensible. The stones were huge and heavy. How could this possibly happen? Herod the Great had refurbished the Temple, he had increased the size of the platform to thirty-five acres. The outer structure had been faced with white stones that shone brightly in the sun. It stood tall. It could be seen for miles. It was magnificent. It was surely indestructible.

The unthinkable

In AD 70, the unthinkable happened. Tired of the constant rebellions of the Jewish freedom fighters (zealots) and with other parts of the Roman Empire causing problems, the order was given to besiege Jerusalem and burn down the Temple. Rome had had enough! The heat from the fire was so ferocious that it melted the gold which seeped through cracks in the stones of the walls. And just as Jesus had foretold, the Temple was ripped apart, the stones were quite literally thrown down as the Roman soldiers took the precious gold.

Thousands of Jews were killed. Others fled and eventually made their way to other nations of the world seeking out a place of safety. They became known as the Diaspora. It was only after the Holocaust of World War Two that Jewish people started to return en masse to Israel once again.

The Diaspora

We will now consider the story of the Diaspora. To visit Israel today is to be confronted by a "salad bowl" of people from around the world! To understand the phenomenon of the recent return from exile of so many Jewish people, it is necessary to hear some of their stories and realize that they have been drawn back to live in Israel by an invisible thread – rather like a homing pigeon finding its way home. It is something supernatural and, as we will learn later, it is something that was foretold in the Bible long ago.

It's one thing to write a dry historical report about what has happened. But, put that report alongside a true story and suddenly we move from black and white into colour! That's what I find so compelling about spending time in Israel and talking to the people who live there – their stories support and confirm what the Bible says about Israel.

4

DANI SAYAG'S STORY

We hear first from Dani Sayag. He is the pastor of a congregation in northern Israel that is based in Haifa. The congregation meet every Shabbat in a village just outside the city called Usfiya on Mount Carmel. Dani is Jewish. He was born in Israel. He will help us understand the history of Israel and will tell us something of what God is doing in Israel today. This is his story:

> We meet at the top of Mt Carmel. It's actually the highest point of the mountain range. The congregation was established in 1991. It started in a drug rehabilitation centre called The House of Victory (Beit Nitzachon in Hebrew) founded by David and Karen Davis when they came to Israel from America. When they started that ministry, they weren't planning to start a congregation as well. But it was just born out of the work and has continued to expand ever since. Today there is a Hebrew-speaking congregation and we've helped to establish an Arabic-speaking congregation – and now it seems God is birthing a Russian-speaking congregation! We don't set a target to start a new congregation; but out of the growth, it just happens.

For many Christians around the world, especially those who have never visited Israel, understanding the relevance of the history of Israel to their lives and appreciating the point in history in which we are now living is something that has never occurred to them. I asked Dani to explain when the story of biblical Israel began.

As I understand, it started with Abraham when God gave him a promise that he was going to bless him and, through him, he would bless all the nations of the world. Even in that promise we see throughout the Scriptures how God then called Isaac and Jacob (later changing Jacob's name to Israel) and God kept that line to the point of when the Messiah came. It's important to understand that God made an unconditional covenant with Abraham. It's not like other covenants in the Bible where God said, "If you will do this, I will do that." In the covenant God made with Abraham, he promised him the land and his blessing over the nation. It was not dependent on the people of Israel keeping God's covenant. God would not change his mind. Rather, he would stay faithful to his covenant. And that's the reason why, when we look at Israel today, it's important to realize the reason the nation has survived exiles and wars is not because Israel did something good. Rather, it's because God is faithful to his promises.

When we look at the history of Israel we can see God's judgment on the nation whether it's through the destruction of the Temple, or sending the Jewish people into exile. But despite their disobedience, God still remained faithful to his people. Even in his wrath. He always remembered his word and showed mercy. The moment God says, "I'm rejecting Israel totally," he would not be faithful to his word. But God is faithful to his word. So we went through a lot of suffering as a chosen people. And I want to tell you, you don't want to be a chosen people because you then become an example. And Israel became an example to show that if you don't follow God's ways, there will be a judgment. But also the blessing applies in the same way; that if you keep God's promises, God is going to bless you. And we see it upon this nation.

"What does it mean to be God's chosen people?" I asked Dani.

It's a hard thing to understand! Being chosen means there is a specific calling that God gave this nation. By restoring this nation again in recent history and in bringing the people back to this land, he did it because there is still a calling, a destiny, on this nation to be a light for the rest of the world. And I believe that when Israel will follow the ways of the Lord it will be an example to the nations. When Israel became a nation again (in 1948) and the odds were against us, God fought for this nation and provided supernatural protection because God has a unique purpose for this nation. For people who are not from Israel who may be asking, so "who am I?", you are also chosen because in Romans 11 we read you have been grafted into the "olive tree", so every blessing God promises to Israel, is also for you. But at the same time we all have to understand that there is a specific calling from God for this nation of Israel and I believe that we are going to see in the future more Jewish people coming to know the Lord. From my understanding of the Bible, in particular in Paul's letter to the Romans, I am expecting there will be a national revival and then the nations of the world will see that God is here in Israel.

Opinion is one thing, but this book is about discovering biblical facts and hearing actual stories that help us to understand modern Israel today. We know from history that in AD 70 the land was sacked by the Romans, and Jewish people fled for their lives and ended up around the world seeking places of safety in which to live and rebuild their lives. But as recent history has also shown, over the past one hundred years in particular – which is almost two thousand years since that third exile in AD 70 – Jewish people have been returning to Israel from the four corners of the world, drawn as it were, by an invisible thread. We have to ask why. I asked Dani whether he could tell me where in the Old Testament it is mentioned that Jewish people would return to live in Israel at this time.

You can read it specifically in the prophets: Ezekiel 36:22–36 is very clear where God says that he will bring us back from the nations to Israel and then he will do a spiritual work in us here.

I am bringing you back, but not because you deserve it. I am doing it to protect my holy name, on which you brought shame while you were scattered among the nations. I will show how holy my great name is – the name on which you brought shame among the nations. And when I reveal my holiness through you before their very eyes, says the Sovereign Lord, then the nations will know that I am the Lord. For I will gather you up from all the nations and bring you home again to your land.

Then I will sprinkle clean water on you, and you will be clean. Your filth will be washed away, and you will no longer worship idols. And I will give you a new heart, and I will put a new spirit in you. I will take out your stony, stubborn heart and give you a tender, responsive heart. And I will put my Spirit in you so that you will follow my decrees and be careful to obey my regulations.

You will live in Israel, the land I gave your ancestors long ago. You will be my people, and I will be your God. I will cleanse you of your filthy behaviour. I will give you good crops of grain, and I will send no more famines on the land. I will give you great harvests from your fruit trees and fields, and never again will the surrounding nations be able to scoff at your land for its famines. Then you will remember your past sins and despise yourselves for all the detestable things you did. But remember, says the Sovereign Lord, I am not doing this because you deserve it. O my people of Israel, you should be utterly ashamed of all you have done!

> *This is what the Sovereign Lord says: When I cleanse you from your sins, I will repopulate your cities, and the ruins will be rebuilt. The fields that used to lie empty and desolate in plain view of everyone will again be farmed. And when I bring you back, people will say, "This former wasteland is now like the Garden of Eden! The abandoned and ruined cities now have strong walls and are filled with people!" Then the surrounding nations that survive will know that I, the Lord, have rebuilt the ruins and replanted the wasteland. For I, the Lord, have spoken, and I will do what I say.*

We can see two stages to this prophecy – the physical restoration of Israel and the spiritual restoration of Israel. Until now we've seen a lot of physical restoration. It's amazing, when you come and visit Israel you will not believe that in just over seventy years God has done and is doing so much. This land used to be like a desert without trees. Even Mark Twain, when he came here before Israel became a nation, describes the land as one of desolation – it was depressing! When you walk in Israel today, it's blossoming. So that's the first part.

But there is a second part where God says he will give them a new heart and will put his Spirit in them and then they will know him. So when I read that I understand they will come here in unbelief and then God will do his work in their hearts in the land of Israel. And we are starting to see that already. We see Jewish people coming to know Jesus, Yeshua, as their Messiah. We see how God is moving among new immigrants. One of the amazing things that has happened is that, since 1991, over a million Russians have come from the former Soviet Union to Israel and it's changed the Body of Messiah in the land. With suddenly so many Russian speakers, we had to change our meetings! We had to have translation into Russian. So we see the people God is bringing – he is touching them and saving them and you can see this in every congregation in Israel.

In 1948, when Israel became a nation once again, there were twenty-three Jewish believers living in the land. Today we number approximately 30,000 – every year there has been an increase. And we believe it's going to continue to grow.

Every year, thousands of new immigrants come to Israel. And today when we look around the world at the rise of anti-Semitism, we see many Jewish people no longer feel safe and they are thinking about coming to the land. I think the next big Aliyah (immigration) we will see will probably come from France.

Later in this book, we will consider in greater detail the events that led to the rebirth of Israel as a nation in 1948. But first, we will continue with the theme of the recent return to Israel of Jewish people who, for centuries, have been living in other nations around the world. How did they manage to maintain their Jewish identity while at the same time assimilating into the culture of the host nation?

In the next chapter, we will consider the story of Solomon – a Jew from Ethiopia.

5

SOLOMON'S STORY: A JEW FROM ETHIOPIA

The history of the Jewish community in Ethiopia goes back approximately one and a half thousand years. There are many stories about how they came to be there but, while there, they developed their own version of Judaism. They called themselves Beta Israel (House of Israel). Others (non-Jews) called them by the derogatory term, falasha, meaning "outsider". Over the centuries, they have experienced persecution and severe hardship. They lived mainly in small villages in northern Ethiopia.

During the late twentieth century, the number of Ethiopian Jews coming to live in Israel increased dramatically. There were two major operations to bring them out of Ethiopia – the first was called Operation Moses (1983–85) when 20,000 men, women, and children were airlifted to Israel; the second was Operation Solomon (May 1991) when just over 14,000 people were brought out of the country to Israel.

Coming from Africa and a non-European culture to live in Israel, has proved challenging for the Ethiopian Jewish community. Solomon's story (not his real name) exemplifies the struggle that many have experienced.

Solomon came to Israel with his mother and siblings in 1990 when he was thirteen years old. In late 2019, we arranged to meet in Haifa, where he lives today with his wife and family. A softly-spoken man, he is serious yet friendly. This is his story:

I was born into a Jewish family and we grew up as a Jewish family in Ethiopia. I knew about my religion (Judaism) from a child because my mum told us that one day we would leave Ethiopia and go to Jerusalem because we're Jewish. So it was just a question of time and we waited for the right time. As Jews, we lived separately from the others. We celebrated all the Jewish feasts and as we waited we prayed to come to Israel. And as God promised, we are now here in Israel.

"When you were young, you knew you were Jewish, so were you part of a close-knit Jewish community?" I asked Solomon.

Mostly, the Ethiopian Jews lived in different villages to other Ethiopians. In each village where we lived, there were synagogues. We had a Torah scroll [a long scroll containing the text of the Five Books of Moses, hand-written by a scribe in Hebrew] and we kept Shabbat [the Sabbath]. So we had a separate life from the others. Other Ethiopians knew about us; they called us falasha which means "a people who flew from a place they do not belong to". We were made to feel apart and separate from mainstream Ethiopian society even though we were the same colour, shared the same culture, ate the same food, and called ourselves Ethiopian. We were considered and treated as being different. There were many other unpleasant names they called us because we were Jewish. It was very hard to live in Ethiopia as Jews – even though we were Ethiopian. And so we lived a different kind of life, waiting and praying to come to Zion.

My grandfather was a rabbi and most of my family were involved with the Jewish community in Ethiopia. While I was waiting to come to Zion, for me being a Jewish person and living in Ethiopia, my dream was to come to Israel and become a rabbi.

Solomon's early life was made suddenly more difficult when his father died. It was after this that Solomon's mother took the decision to leave Ethiopia and bring her children to Israel.

"How did they travel and what route did they take," I asked. He continued:

There were two big Aliyahs [immigrations] from Ethiopia. One was Operation Moses in 1984, through Sudan. The second one, in 1991, was called Operation Solomon. But our Aliyah was between these two. We flew from Ethiopia to Greece. We spent one night in Greece and then we were taken by bus to an airport where we boarded an El Al plane and a few hours later we found ourselves in Israel instead of the US! We were very surprised because when we left Ethiopia we were told we had documents to fly to the US. We came to Greece and then found ourselves in Israel!

What was his reaction on finding himself as a thirteen-year-old arriving in Israel rather than America?

Well, it was very exciting at that time because it was a dream come true – especially for my family. When we landed at the airport and realized we were in Israel, most of the Ethiopian Jews who came with us, kissed the ground and we thanked God for that moment. The night we arrived, we were driven to the northern part of Israel to a reception centre where we stayed for one year to learn the language and understand what life would be like in Israel.

"How hard was it for you to settle and feel at home here?"

It was very hard because we came from a completely different culture and a different lifestyle. Most of the Ethiopian Jews came from a farming background. They were not educated. They lived their life in a good way in Ethiopia, but to come to a western lifestyle meant adapting to a different way of living where everything is fast, where everybody has the opportunity to go to school and receive an education, and there's a new language to learn. Even the food was different. It was a big shock – still is! We are still dealing with that even after thirty years in Israel!

On reaching the age of eighteen, Solomon, like the majority of Israelis, joined the army (Israeli Defence Force) to serve his obligatory three years. I wondered whether that experience helped him to integrate fully into Israeli life.

The army is challenging for everybody in Israel! But for those of us from Ethiopia, the army is the place where we feel equal. You can even learn life skills that will help you in the future. So for me, it was a place where I learned a lot of things. I felt equal to other Israelis. For me it was a place of safety.

Solomon had told me that his ambition was to become a rabbi in Israel like his grandfather had been in Ethiopia – so what part was religion playing in his life at this time? "You say you came from a traditional Jewish background, you celebrated the feasts and read the Torah. What about when you came to Israel?" I asked him.

After I came to Israel, I went to a boarding school for three years. It was a Yeshiva, a religious school for Orthodox Jews. And as I told you, my dream was to become a rabbi. So at first it was good for me. But after three years, I had many questions, and the challenge of the Orthodox religious lifestyle was becoming too heavy for me. After I finished my time in the army, I was working in Eilat and I met three people who talked about Yeshua. For me, it was very bad to hear about Yeshua in Israel because as Jews we had suffered from the Christians in Ethiopia – so my response was, "Sorry, it's not for me."

Soon after that encounter I came to visit my family in Nazareth, which is where we were living then, and I met two people and again they talked about Yeshua with me. They invited me to a conference at Yad Hashmona [a conference centre near Jerusalem]. It was a three-day conference. So there I was! Even now, when I remember what happened there I feel excited. On the second day, it was a Friday, there was a prayer time and the pastor invited people for prayer. For some reason, he came up to me and asked me why I was there! I was not ready for such a question, but I told him I wanted to know who was the right Messiah in Israel. As he started to pray for me suddenly I saw water, oil, and wind coming towards me very strongly and fast. It touched my face and I fell down. And from that moment I understood that Yeshua is my Saviour. Yeshua is my Messiah. And not just for me, but for all Jewish people. And from that day I have followed Yeshua as my Saviour. And I am so happy about that.

It's amazing that it happened so quickly because for many Jewish people it can be a long process understanding who the Messiah really is. I see it as a pastor now, how it's not easy for some people. But sometimes, the way God meets with people is different. I compare my experience on meeting Jesus with the Apostle Paul because suddenly, in a moment, he changed my life. He convinced me that he is my Saviour – and he has his plan for my life. It was a different experience, but for me it's something that has guided my life from that moment until now and I'm so excited to talk about Yeshua.

"Suddenly you realized you weren't going to become a rabbi," I said.

Yes, but I think I've become a rabbi in a different way! Now is the time when we say, "Baruch Haba B'shem Adonai" – "Blessed is he who comes in the name of the Lord." After a gap of 2,000 years, we are back in Israel. We have come back to our land after being outside. We say those words every Shabbat, "Baruch Haba B'shem Adonai." It's a big miracle for me that I accepted Yeshua here in Israel. In Ethiopia, I learned all about Judaism, but after I came to Israel, I met Yeshua. It's a big miracle for me. I was not influenced by Christians, but I was touched by the Holy Spirit and it is powerful for me.

Solomon's life changed at the conference at Yad Hashmona. He then knew that he wanted to study and, after being granted a place at university, he came to Haifa to begin his first degree.

I studied Special Education for my first degree. I would say that when I met Yeshua, he changed my life and my mind because I didn't plan to go to university at that time. But the moment I met Yeshua, he changed not only my life but my thinking. So I came to Haifa for my first degree. While studying at the university I met my wife – we were in the same tutorial group. One day the other students in the group asked me why I was "different". So I started to share about Yeshua.

When I first met my future wife she was suffering from frequent headaches which meant she had to keep going to the hospital. She told me, if your Messiah, your Yeshua is real, I want to check him out through my health. If he can change my life and heal me of these headaches, he can change everything. So I told her, we can pray. As we started to pray, she fell down and from that moment she was healed. The Jewish people want to see a sign! So she accepted Yeshua and after three years we got married. She is from Ethiopia also.

At that time I knew ten or fifteen other believers from Ethiopia. Today, there are now more than 1,000 of us spread around the country, so that's a real breakthrough.

Solomon finished his degree and started working for the Haifa municipality where his job involves him in planning a programme for teenagers to help those struggling with drug and alcohol addiction.

We have a challenge amongst the younger generation here with alcohol and drug addiction. I have written a project for them. It was a mission for me. There are many Ethiopians with this problem in Haifa. For me, it was an opportunity to meet them through this project and even to share my life story with them – "before Yeshua" and "after Yeshua". We see how things change – it takes time, it's a process. But we see fruit with that project also. We have a big challenge with the new generation of young Ethiopians, 40 per cent of whom were born in Israel. All they know is Israel. They think as Israelis. But we are a different colour. To live a life where there is racism and prejudice as a young person born in Israel, where they have known no other way of life, they don't understand it. How do they deal with racism? Eleven young Ethiopians have been killed by the police in recent times for no reason. The last one, Solomon Tekah, he lived in Haifa. I knew him. I know his family. He was a young person who was thinking about his future. He was preparing to go into the army. And his life was finished in one second by shooting. So you can imagine what kind of feeling this caused amongst the young generation of Ethiopians who consider themselves Israelis. So they are fighting for their life. There were two days of demonstrations in Israel as a result of Solomon Tekah's death and it was very hard. But it comes as a result of hurt feelings and a burning anger. So it's very tough. That's why as believers we pray for this situation because I believe we need the hand of God in these kind of problems.

Solomon is working full time. He and his wife also have four children so their life is busy. However, they felt God was calling them to start a congregation. How did that happen?

As soon as Yeshua met with me on that day, that changed my life – I knew he had a special thing for me to do. I prayed a lot with others who also recognized this. In 2008, another pastor encouraged me to be ordained as a pastor and to start the congregation. From that time, we have seen people come to faith and seen the congregation grow. We have young people and old people in the congregation. There are about 100 people now. We know of other Ethiopians who know about Yeshua but they are afraid to come to the congregation because of their families. One of the tough things for Ethiopian believers is our community. Many are ultra-Orthodox religious Jews and they are fanatic and it's very hard for us to deal with. It's just by his grace. We have had many situations when the Ethiopian rabbi has declared that any Ethiopian Jews who believe in Yeshua can be killed. They say we are not under the law of the Israeli Government, we are under the law of God. So to be an Ethiopian Jew believing in Yeshua is very tough.

Our congregation is not just for Ethiopians. My vision, as a person who grew up in Israel and speaks Hebrew very well, is to see all aspects of discrimination destroyed. The gospel is not coloured. All of us accept Yeshua as our Father. So my vision is to see our congregation with different colours. To the young people, we speak only in Hebrew. We only speak Amharic to the older generation who cannot speak or understand Hebrew easily. We have Israeli Arabs in our congregation as well. We are a mixed Jewish/Arab congregation. And we have a ministry to help needy families. We have twenty families, none of them are believers, but they have heard about Yeshua and fifteen of these families are Arabs, some are Muslim. We want to impact all the community because Yeshua is the good news for all of us. We are open to all people to show them the love of God.

"How have you managed to grow so quickly despite the difficulties you have faced?" I asked Solomon.

There are three reasons. Firstly, we try to show our love to the community and we talk about Yeshua – the one from whom our love is coming. It's not because we are good but because God loves us. The second reason is, we have an evangelism group and they go out twice a week in Haifa to share the gospel. The third thing is, the Lord shows his faithfulness with wonders and miracles. So people get healed. People get delivered from demonic spirits. And then these people go and share with their families what God has done for them. They in turn come to see what's going on and they also get healed! So, when people share what's happened to them, they bring others and they come to know Yeshua too.

We have many young people in our congregation. Some of them have high positions in the army. They have a vision for this nation, for the younger generation. And for us as Ethiopians, another mission is to destroy this spirit of racism and discrimination. We can make it as children of God, by his power. Our young people have God's power in their lives and we want to show God's love to the people. We have a meeting twice a week that brings all the young people together to worship God. It's very special.

Solomon's story is one example among thousands that could be shared in this book, stories of Jewish people who have left the nation where their family has lived for generations to come and live in Israel. No other nation has been exiled from its land three times only to return and resume life as that nation again. So what is it that makes Israel unique?

This book is about understanding modern Israel from a biblical point of view. So now we have to consider where in the Bible it talks about exiles returning. That is the subject of our next chapter.

6

WHEN GOD SPOKE TO THE PROPHETS

It is at this point that we have to make a conscious decision to ask a fundamental question, if we truly desire to understand modern Israel from a biblical perspective. That question is simply this, "What is God doing in Israel today?" With so much news coming out of the region covering the ongoing political situation on both secular and Christian news channels, it takes a certain amount of determination to seek out the truth! How sad it is that so many Christians take sides when discussing the rights and wrongs (in their opinion!) of the situation "on the ground". As if our opinions matter! With so much talk of social and political justice in the church today, is there a danger that we only see and therefore consider things from our own limited world view?

We have already covered the early story of Israel and, from the Scriptures and with the benefit of hindsight, we can see clearly that what God foretold regarding the first and second exiles happened just as he predicted through the Bible prophets. It is therefore fair to assume that as those predictions happened just as God foretold, down to the finest details, then prophecies concerning the future final return of Jewish people to the land of Israel would happen accurately too.

In order to find answers to that simple, almost naive question, "What is God doing in Israel today?", we therefore have to familiarize ourselves with some relevant Scriptures. And there are plenty to choose from! We will now look at some of those prophecies and then look for evidence of their fulfilment.

This will help us to unravel the complex situation that is Israel and see this tiny nation through God's eyes rather than our own blurred vision!

One of the books in the Bible that helps to answer this question was written by the Old Testament prophet Isaiah. Writing between 740–680 BC, he prophesied this:

> *In that day the Lord will reach out his hand a second time to bring back the remnant of his people – those who remain in Assyria and northern Egypt; in southern Egypt, Ethiopia, and Elam; in Babylonia, Hamath, and all the distant coastlands.*
> ISAIAH 11:11

Jeremiah, who wrote during the period from 627–580 BC, prophesied that the Jews would be captive in Babylon for seventy years:

> *This is what the Lord says: "You will be in Babylon for seventy years. But then I will come and do for you all the good things I have promised, and I will bring you home again."*
> JEREMIAH 29:10

And Ezra (a scribe, well versed in the law) confirmed this was true when he wrote,

> *In the first year of King Cyrus of Persia, the Lord fulfilled the prophecy he had given through Jeremiah. He stirred the heart of Cyrus to put this proclamation in writing and to send it throughout his kingdom:*
>
> *"This is what King Cyrus of Persia says:*
>
> *'The Lord, the God of heaven, has given me all the kingdoms of the earth. He has appointed me to build him a Temple at Jerusalem, which is in Judah. Any of you who are his*

people may go to Jerusalem in Judah to rebuild this Temple of the Lord, the God of Israel, who lives in Jerusalem. And may your God be with you! Wherever this Jewish remnant is found, let their neighbours contribute toward their expenses by giving them silver and gold, supplies for the journey, and livestock, as well as a voluntary offering for the Temple of God in Jerusalem.'"

EZRA 1:1–4

The first year of King Cyrus was 538 BC – seventy years after Jeremiah's prophecy that the Jewish people would first return from Babylon to Israel. But let us return to Isaiah's prophecy which refers to a future return, or a second return to the land of Israel. This is the return that we are concerned with now; the return that began in the last century and is ongoing today.

So that brings us to another question: what happened in the land of Israel after AD 70 when the Roman army sacked the Temple in Jerusalem and largely emptied the land of Jewish people, leaving the country desolate for the next 2,000 years? Where did the Jewish people go? Isaiah's prophecy concerning the "second return" mentioned they would be coming from "the nations". Jeremiah's prophecy tells us more about this:

"But the time is coming," says the Lord, "when people who are taking an oath will no longer say, 'As surely as the Lord lives, who rescued the people of Israel from the land of Egypt.' Instead, they will say, 'As surely as the Lord lives, who brought the people of Israel back to their own land from the land of the north and from all the countries to which he had exiled them.' For I will bring them back to this land that I gave their ancestors."

JEREMIAH 16:14–15

"I will be found by you," says the Lord. "I will end your captivity and restore your fortunes. I will gather you out of

the nations where I sent you and will bring you home again to your own land."
JEREMIAH 29:14

"In that day," says the Lord, "I will be the God of all the families of Israel, and they will be my people." This is what the Lord says:

"Those who survive the coming destruction will find blessings even in the barren land, for I will give rest to the people of Israel."

Long ago the Lord said to Israel: "I have loved you, my people, with an everlasting love. With unfailing love I have drawn you to myself. I will rebuild you, my virgin Israel. You will again be happy and dance merrily with your tambourines. Again you will plant your vineyards on the mountains of Samaria and eat from your own gardens there. The day will come when watchmen will shout from the hill country of Ephraim, 'Come, let us go up to Jerusalem to worship the Lord our God.'"

Now this is what the Lord says: "Sing with joy for Israel. Shout for the greatest of nations! Shout out with praise and joy: 'Save your people, O Lord, the remnant of Israel!' For I will bring them from the north and from the distant corners of the earth. I will not forget the blind and lame, the expectant mothers and women in labour. A great company will return! Tears of joy will stream down their faces, and I will lead them home with great care. They will walk beside quiet streams and on smooth paths where they will not stumble. For I am Israel's father, and Ephraim is my oldest child.

"Listen to this message from the Lord, you nations of the world; proclaim it in distant coastlands: The Lord, who scattered his people, will gather them and watch over them

as a shepherd does his flock. For the Lord has redeemed Israel from those too strong for them. They will come home and sing songs of joy on the heights of Jerusalem. They will be radiant because of the Lord's good gifts – the abundant crops of grain, new wine, and olive oil, and the healthy flocks and herds. Their life will be like a watered garden, and all their sorrows will be gone. The young women will dance for joy, and the men – old and young – will join in the celebration. I will turn their mourning into joy. I will comfort them and exchange their sorrow for rejoicing. The priests will enjoy abundance, and my people will feast on my good gifts. I, the Lord, have spoken!"

This is what the Lord says: "A cry is heard in Ramah – deep anguish and bitter weeping. Rachel weeps for her children, refusing to be comforted – for her children are gone."

But now this is what the Lord says: "Do not weep any longer, for I will reward you," says the Lord. "Your children will come back to you from the distant land of the enemy. There is hope for your future," says the Lord. "Your children will come again to their own land. I have heard Israel saying, 'You disciplined me severely, like a calf that needs training for the yoke. Turn me again to you and restore me, for you alone are the Lord my God. I turned away from God, but then I was sorry. I kicked myself for my stupidity! I was thoroughly ashamed of all I did in my younger days.'

"Is not Israel still my son, my darling child?" says the Lord. "I often have to punish him, but I still love him. That's why I long for him and surely will have mercy on him. Set up road signs; put up guideposts. Mark well the path by which you came. Come back again, my virgin Israel; return to your towns here. How long will you wander, my wayward daughter? For the Lord will cause something new to happen – Israel will embrace her God."

This is what the Lord of Heaven's Armies, the God of Israel, says: "When I bring them back from captivity, the people of Judah and its towns will again say, 'The Lord bless you, O righteous home, O holy mountain!' Townspeople and farmers and shepherds alike will live together in peace and happiness. For I have given rest to the weary and joy to the sorrowing."

At this, I woke up and looked around. My sleep had been very sweet.

"The day is coming," says the Lord, "when I will greatly increase the human population and the number of animals here in Israel and Judah. In the past I deliberately uprooted and tore down this nation. I overthrew it, destroyed it, and brought disaster upon it. But in the future I will just as deliberately plant it and build it up. I, the Lord, have spoken!

"The people will no longer quote this proverb: 'The parents have eaten sour grapes, but their children's mouths pucker at the taste.' All people will die for their own sins – those who eat the sour grapes will be the ones whose mouths will pucker.

"The day is coming," says the Lord, "when I will make a new covenant with the people of Israel and Judah. This covenant will not be like the one I made with their ancestors when I took them by the hand and brought them out of the land of Egypt. They broke that covenant, though I loved them as a husband loves his wife," says the Lord.

"But this is the new covenant I will make with the people of Israel after those days," says the Lord. "I will put my instructions deep within them, and I will write them on their hearts. I will be their God, and they will be my people. And they will not need to teach their neighbours, nor will they need to teach their relatives, saying, 'You should know

the Lord.' For everyone, from the least to the greatest, will know me already," says the Lord. "And I will forgive their wickedness, and I will never again remember their sins."

It is the Lord who provides the sun to light the day and the moon and stars to light the night, and who stirs the sea into roaring waves. His name is the Lord of Heaven's Armies, and this is what he says: "I am as likely to reject my people Israel as I am to abolish the laws of nature!" This is what the Lord says: "Just as the heavens cannot be measured and the foundations of the earth cannot be explored, so I will not consider casting them away for the evil they have done. I, the Lord, have spoken!

"The day is coming," says the Lord, "when all Jerusalem will be rebuilt for me, from the Tower of Hananel to the Corner Gate. A measuring line will be stretched out over the hill of Gareb and across to Goah. And the entire area – including the graveyard and ash dump in the valley, and all the fields out to the Kidron Valley on the east as far as the Horse Gate – will be holy to the Lord. The city will never again be captured or destroyed."

JEREMIAH 31:1–40

I would like to suggest that this dramatic chapter of Jeremiah not only explains that the Lord will bring the Jewish people back to Israel from the nations of the world, it also demonstrates his heart towards them! Here we feel the pain of a father whose children have turned away from him and his longing to have them return home where they belong.

There are so many references to this final return, too many to include in this short book. But we should include another part of Isaiah's prophecy here:

"Do not be afraid, for I am with you. I will gather you and your children from east and west. I will say to the north and south, 'Bring my sons and daughters back to Israel from the distant corners of the earth.'"
ISAIAH 43:5–6

So has it happened just as God said through the Scriptures we have just read? The answer is of course a resounding, "Yes!" It is interesting to study the demographic development of Palestine (as the Romans renamed the land in AD 70) to the Israel of today. For example, in AD 1517 there were 5,000 Jews living in the land and 295,000 non-Jews (1.7 per cent of the population being Jewish). In 1882, the number of Jews living in Palestine numbered 24,000 with non-Jews numbering 276,000, giving a total population of 300,000 (8 per cent of whom were Jewish). By the end of 2019, the numbers of Jewish people living in Israel had risen to almost 7 million, the total population had risen to over 9 million (74 per cent of whom are Jewish). (These figures do not include the West Bank or Gaza).

Understanding modern Israel

Of course, to understand modern Israel, you really have to go there! And one place to visit in order to better see and understand where Jewish people have lived around the world, secreted in the nations, is the Museum of the Jewish People in Tel Aviv at Beit Hatfutsot.

As they say themselves, "It's not just about exhibitions. We offer a large variety of lectures on Jewish culture, Jewish languages, Jewish genealogy, Israeli and Jewish documentary films, and many other fascinating topics." To wander around this museum is to realize Jews have come back to Israel from Iraq, Morocco, Ethiopia, Western and Eastern Europe, Russia, and India, to name but a few!

Why has God brought the Jewish people back to Israel?

We have followed the biblical thread of exile and return. Now we have to ask, "Why?" What is the reason God has for gathering the Jewish people together at this time in history? There are many places in the Bible where the answer to this question can be clearly found:

> *He will raise a flag among the nations and assemble the exiles of Israel. He will gather the scattered people of Judah from the ends of the earth.*
>
> ISAIAH 11:12

> *This is what the Sovereign Lord says: The people of Israel will again live in their own land, the land I gave my servant Jacob. For I will gather them from the distant lands where I have scattered them. I will reveal to the nations of the world my holiness among my people.*
>
> EZEKIEL 28:25

Can we therefore understand from the above verses that the regathering of Israel is not just about Israel, it is about God revealing who he is to the nations of the world through Israel? This is the bigger picture that we need to concern ourselves with now. How is God going to work through this tiny nation to achieve his purposes to reveal himself to the nations of the world in these days in which we are now living? But before we answer that question there is another matter we need to understand and that concerns another major reason why God has acted to rebuild the nation of Israel and reinhabit it with Jewish people once again now. The answer to this question can be found in the book of the prophet Ezekiel.

So who was Ezekiel?

The opening verses of the book of Ezekiel tell us he was a priest who at the age of thirty found himself an exile in Babylon during the fifth year of King Jehoiachin's captivity.

> *On July 31 of my thirtieth year, while I was with the Judean exiles beside the River Kebar in Babylon, the heavens were opened and I saw visions of God. This happened during the fifth year of King Jehoiachin's captivity. (The Lord gave this message to Ezekiel son of Buzi, a priest, beside the River Kebar in the land of the Babylonians, and he felt the hand of the Lord take hold of him.)*
>
> EZEKIEL 1:1–3

From this information, historians have deduced Ezekiel would have been thirty in 593 BC and would have been part of the second deportation to Babylon in 597 BC when Nebuchadnezzar attacked Jerusalem for the second time and took 10,000 Jewish people hostage. In other words, he was born in 622 BC, deported to Babylon in 597 BC and his prophetic ministry began in 592 BC until approximately 570 BC. (Daniel had been taken to Babylon in the first deportation in 605 BC and as Ezekiel mentions him three times in his book we can be sure he was familiar with what Daniel was saying.)

The messages God gave Ezekiel to share with the Jews in exile were a combination of judgment but also hope. Having already discussed the return of the exiles from Babylon (the second exile) earlier in this book, it is the promise of the future restoration of Israel that we will concern ourselves with here. And here Ezekiel's prophecy, written 2,500 years ago comes alive to us today as we look at what has been happening in Israel particularly since 1948.

> *Therefore, give the people of Israel this message from the Sovereign Lord: I am bringing you back, but not because you*

deserve it. I am doing it to protect my holy name, on which you brought shame while you were scattered among the nations. I will show how holy my great name is – the name on which you brought shame among the nations. And when I reveal my holiness through you before their very eyes, says the Sovereign Lord, then the nations will know that I am the Lord. For I will gather you up from all the nations and bring you home again to your land.

Then I will sprinkle clean water on you, and you will be clean. Your filth will be washed away, and you will no longer worship idols. And I will give you a new heart, and I will put a new spirit in you. I will take out your stony, stubborn heart and give you a tender, responsive heart. And I will put my Spirit in you so that you will follow my decrees and be careful to obey my regulations.

And you will live in Israel, the land I gave your ancestors long ago. You will be my people, and I will be your God. I will cleanse you of your filthy behaviour. I will give you good crops of grain, and I will send no more famines on the land. I will give you great harvests from your fruit trees and fields, and never again will the surrounding nations be able to scoff at your land for its famines. Then you will remember your past sins and despise yourselves for all the detestable things you did. But remember, says the Sovereign Lord, I am not doing this because you deserve it. O my people of Israel, you should be utterly ashamed of all you have done!

This is what the Sovereign Lord says: When I cleanse you from your sins, I will repopulate your cities, and the ruins will be rebuilt. The fields that used to lie empty and desolate in plain view of everyone will again be farmed. And when I bring you back, people will say, "This former wasteland is now like the Garden of Eden! The abandoned and ruined cities now have strong walls and are filled with people!" Then the surrounding nations that survive will know that I, the Lord, have rebuilt the ruins and replanted the wasteland. For I, the Lord, have spoken, and I will do what I say.

This is what the Sovereign Lord says: I am ready to hear Israel's prayers and to increase their numbers like a flock. They will be as numerous as the sacred flocks that fill Jerusalem's streets at the time of her festivals. The ruined cities will be crowded with people once more, and everyone will know that I am the Lord.

EZEKIEL 36:22–38

It seems clear that the reason God has brought the Jewish people back to the land of Israel is not because of anything they have done to deserve it, but rather to protect the honour of his holy name so that the nations will know the Lord.

All the world will know that I, the Lord, am your Saviour and your Redeemer, the Mighty One of Israel.

ISAIAH 49:26

Now we are certainly engaging with the bigger picture!

But before we jump too far ahead in this story, we need to consider a dark period in history, namely the Holocaust. After two thousand years of being stateless, just as it seemed the Jewish people were starting to move back to their ancient homeland, why did Hitler come to power and want to annihilate the Jewish people? We will hear some stories from this terrible time in world history and consider why this happened.

7

THE HOLOCAUST

It is not the purpose of this book to give an in-depth description of what happened in the Holocaust – one of the darkest periods of European history that, even after seventy plus years, still casts a long shadow.

There are many excellent books on the subject and Yad Vashem, the World Holocaust Remembrance Centre in Jerusalem, provides a detailed, graphic and poignant memorial and reminder to us all of what happened.

When did the Holocaust start? On 30 January 1933, Adolf Hitler was appointed German chancellor and gradually persecution against the Jews and other "undesirables" began, followed by a sustained period of purposeful genocide which gradually ended after VE (Victory in Europe) Day on 8 May 1945. Six million European Jews (as well as millions of others, including gypsies and homosexuals) were murdered by the German Nazi regime during the Second World War.

If it was an attempt by dark spiritual forces working through Adolf Hitler and the Nazis to annihilate Jewish people from the face of the earth, then it didn't work. Rather, despite the appalling loss of life and indescribable suffering, out of the ashes, Israel was reborn in 1948. We will come on to tell that story in the next chapter of this book.

It is the human stories, the stories of survival that we will now explore – people like Anna.

Anna's story

Now an elderly lady living in an apartment in Ariel, a city in the centre of Israel, I was taken to meet her by David and Leah Ortiz in April 2017. Anna survived the Holocaust – many years later, she agreed to share her story. David and Leah were there to interpret and it was clear from the beginning that this was going to be a painful experience for Anna.

She began with her earliest memories – although they were not memories at all, rather she was recounting what her mother had told her. Anna had such a traumatic start in life, she has no memories of that time.

My first memories begin after the war. I was born in a ghetto in Ukraine in 1942. What I know about my life in the ghetto was told to me by my mother. I don't remember the war at all – I have no memory of that time.

My parents were Jews from Moldova. They were made to walk from Moldova to the ghetto in Ukraine. It was 35 degrees centigrade. They didn't let them eat or drink. On the way many died. Many were killed. They could only eat what they found on the ground. They were not given any food or water. Whatever they found in the fields they ate, without cooking anything.

There was a building in the Ukraine where they took a number of teenage boys onto the roof and they took pot shots at them. It was like a game; some were killed, others were wounded. One of the boys was wounded in both his legs and then they shot him dead.

My parents had a traditional Jewish wedding in Moldova which was part of Romania before the Soviets came and took over. The Soviets didn't recognize the Jewish wedding and so, a few years later, my parents had to get married again in a civic ceremony in the city hall. By then they had a boy who was seven and a half years old but, even so, the Soviets did not recognize they were already married. My grandparents arranged a party to celebrate this second wedding and they (the Soviet soldiers) took everybody from the house who had been at the party and put them into a field intending to kill them. However, when the Bishop heard about this, he came from the church and intervened for them and told the Soviets, "These people are good people, why are you going to kill them? If you kill them, then kill me together with them." They allowed them to go but then a little later sent them on the march in 1941. And on that march, my mother was pregnant with me. My brother, their first child, died on the march.

They separated the family, aunts and uncles and cousins; all were sent in different directions. There was one particular settlement where they took all the Jews and put them into a church. My father recalled how they had had nothing to eat or drink on the journey and were extremely weak; he remembered how their lives were saved by a German soldier who, after making sure nobody was looking, threw a package of bread and sugar to the starving group of Jews. Each one took a little piece and that's how they stayed alive before continuing to walk forward on this march. They walked from place to place. They let them sleep but only for a couple of hours and that was on the ground.

My mother later told me about some of the dreadful atrocities she had witnessed. After they killed the young people on the rooftop, a little later, a German soldier took a baby and tore him apart and threw him into a puddle of water then made everybody drink some of the water.

There was an elderly rabbi in the group and it was the Day of Atonement and they hadn't given them any food for days. But on this day, they gave them bread and coffee. Nobody wanted to eat because it was the Day of Atonement – a day when Jewish people fast – and the Germans told the rabbi to start praying. He started to pray and they beat him. He stopped praying and they beat him some more until he died.

When they got to the ghetto, they put them into a cow

shed with a dirt floor. They had a little bit of hay to make pillows. Some died. Others were raped. Others were killed. Germans and Romanians were both involved in this – they were both living in this city.

I was born in 1942 – I don't know the exact date I was born. Gentile Ukrainians came into the ghetto and the Jews would trade with them; if one had a ring they would trade with them for a piece of bread.

Suddenly, my mother went into labour. The Ukrainians wore long skirts, with large petticoats underneath. One of the Ukrainians took off her slip and cut it into pieces and helped my mother to give birth. She wrapped me in pieces of material. She wanted to take me out of the ghetto but my mother told her she had already lost one child and she wasn't going to give me away. For three years, I never cried and I never spoke. My mother said even the dogs in the streets didn't make a noise in that place – there was such fear in the air. She tied me to her stomach with rags and that's where I grew, in the darkness under her skirt. This Ukrainian came to nurse me because my mother didn't have enough strength in her body to nurse me. The woman who was nursing me gave me my name, Anna.

In 1943, they closed the ghetto completely – they didn't let anybody in and they didn't let anybody out and that's when things got really bad. The dead lay next to the living – nobody removed the bodies. My mother no longer had any strength. Everybody told my mother to throw me away because I didn't have a voice – I didn't speak or cry. But my mother said, "No. She will live with me and I with her." She was almost dead.

Eventually, the Russian army arrived and had victory over the Germans and Romanians. The Russian soldiers entered the ghetto and they started to remove all the dead bodies. When they reached my mother, she was so weak and thin they thought she was a dead body. But when they touched her she made a slight noise so they took her to a hospital and there they found me tied to her stomach.

It was in the hospital that my mother was reunited with her sister. They hadn't seen each other for many years. My mother had nothing to keep her warm but her sister had two blankets. So the nurses took one of her blankets and gave it to my mother and there they remained together. Because of the extreme cold my mother's sister had lost half of her leg.

After some time, when they had recovered sufficiently, the Russians told them to go home and they walked out of the hospital and started to walk the long journey home.

They went to the train station and it was packed with people – everybody was trying to go home.

When the Russians came and liberated them from the ghetto, they immediately took my father away to fight with the Russian army. He eventually arrived home in 1946.

Meanwhile, the train arrived but it was totally full. There was no room for anybody else. Then, all of a sudden, for the first time in my life I began to scream and cry. My mother realized this was a sign that she had to get on the train. Somehow she managed to squeeze us into a carriage and no sooner had the train left the station and travelled a short distance before the platform where we had been standing was bombed and people who had been left there were killed. If we hadn't got on that train, we too would have died.

From that time, my mother told me God loved me and she believed my crying on that day had been a sign from God that she had to get on that train. These are all my mother's stories. I don't remember any of this. She told me many, many, very difficult and bad stories that I can't even repeat.

My own memories start at the point when we reached our village – there was nothing left of our house and the house where my grandparents had lived was so badly damaged there were only three walls and half a roof remaining. But at least it was something and it was there we began living. I remember my father coming back from the army in 1946 and he had a very long beard. I remember seeing him, and calling to my mother, "A bear is coming!"

I remember beginning to understand this was my father. I remember how hard things were, and often we had no food. My father began to rebuild the house in this Romanian town. Moldova was now part of Romania; the Russians had Moldova and the rest was Romania. Two languages were spoken and I learned both and would interpret for my mother. We spoke Yiddish in the house. My mother was a seamstress and had many Romanian customers which is how I learned Romanian. So I spoke three languages at that time – Yiddish, Romanian, and Russian. I later became a teacher of the Russian language and now I speak Hebrew too!

My parents had higher education but when the Russians came they were left, as it were, without any education. My father was a very religious man but everything he had studied and learned was in Yiddish. He was a tailor and that's how they made their living because they didn't have a language.

We wanted to come to Israel in the 1970s but eventually came in 1996. In 1994, my younger brother had already made Aliyah. In 1995, my daughter came. And in 1996 , me, my parents, and my son came. I have two children. I had three brothers and they all survived the war.

In the 1970s, when we wanted to make Aliyah, my husband's mother would not sign the necessary paperwork for him. At that time it caused problems between us and we divorced. Because we divorced and our house belonged to the state, we were thrown out and for five years I was unable to work. I lived with my parents and they fed me and my children. The state offered to hire me to tell stories against Israel in return for payment. I told them, "If you let me go to Israel and let me see what goes on there, I will come back and tell you stories. How can I tell stories about something I know nothing about?" It was always on the radio telling bad stories about Israel – how they were horrible to the Palestinians. It was on radio and TV all the time. And they wanted me to participate in that. But I didn't want to.

In 1996, you didn't need any paperwork and they allowed whoever wanted to go, to go to Israel. But you couldn't take anything with you – we came with only two suitcases.

My daughter was twenty-one when she made Aliyah and when I came here with my son he was eighteen and after six months he was inducted into the army.

We had a big apartment in Moldova with five rooms and a big kitchen and we sold it for 5,000 dollars. The Gentiles who bought it would only pay that amount. That provided us with exactly one year's rent in Israel. I didn't sit in the house and wait for national insurance to support me. I worked very hard. I cleaned houses. I worked with elderly people. I took care of little children. I didn't just sit around and wait for God to provide for me. I was fifty-six when we came here. My father was almost blind. My mother was paralysed in her hands and legs and couldn't even drink water by herself.

We came to Ariel to live. After one year, I bought this apartment where we are sitting now. When I first came to Israel I was renting an apartment but the landlord wouldn't even allow us to put curtains at the windows. So one day I went outside and stood next to the synagogue. I said to God I didn't want anything except for my own house. I took a mortgage and a loan and slowly we managed to build a life here.

In a little while, there is not going to be anybody left to tell these stories. My mother was very smart: she said the story of what happened in the Holocaust has to be passed on from generation to generation so such a thing would not happen again.

I'm a Jew from the beginning to the end. It's very difficult for me to share these memories.

We later heard that Anna didn't sleep for three nights after our meeting.

The Holocaust was the most appalling atrocity. Yet, just a few years after the end of the Second World War something happened that shook the world and its reverberations are ongoing: Israel was reborn when, on 14 May 1948, David Ben-Gurion secretly and suddenly gathered his cabinet in a room in Tel Aviv. They hurriedly drafted the new constitution and declared to the world that Israel was now an independent state!

We will now explore what happened and why and whether or not this was prophesied in the Bible. It is time to understand modern Israel.

8

ISRAEL'S REBIRTH IN 1948

Who has ever seen anything as strange as this? Who ever heard of such a thing? Has a nation ever been born in a single day? Has a country ever come forth in a mere moment?
ISAIAH 66:8

These words of Isaiah were written in 700 BC and they were fulfilled nearly two thousand seven hundred years later when, on 14 May 1948, the British mandate over Palestine ended. A meeting was hurriedly arranged in secret for the Jewish People's Council to gather at the Tel Aviv Museum to approve a proclamation declaring the establishment of the State of Israel. Invitations were sent out to invited dignitaries and, at the appointed time, each took their seat in the crowded room.

David Ben-Gurion rose to his feet and read the following declaration to the gathered assembly:

ERETZ-ISRAEL [(Hebrew) – the Land of Israel] was the birthplace of the Jewish people. Here their spiritual, religious and political identity was shaped. Here they first attained to statehood, created cultural values of national and universal significance and gave to the world the eternal Book of Books. After being forcibly exiled from their land, the people kept faith with it throughout their Dispersion and never ceased to pray and hope for their return to it and for the restoration in it of their political freedom.

Impelled by this historic and traditional attachment, Jews strove in every successive generation to re-establish themselves in their ancient homeland. In recent decades they returned in their masses. Pioneers, ma'pilim [(Hebrew) – immigrants coming to Eretz-Israel in defiance of restrictive legislation] and defenders, they made deserts bloom, revived the Hebrew language, built villages and towns, and created a thriving community controlling its own economy and culture, loving peace but knowing how to defend itself, bringing the blessings of progress to all the country's inhabitants, and aspiring towards independent nationhood.

In the year 5657 (1897), at the summons of the spiritual father of the Jewish State, Theodore Herzl, the First Zionist Congress convened and proclaimed the right of the Jewish people to national rebirth in its own country.

This right was recognized in the Balfour Declaration of the 2nd November, 1917, and reaffirmed in the Mandate of the League of Nations which, in particular, gave international sanction to the historic connection between the Jewish people and Eretz-Israel and to the right of the Jewish people to rebuild its National Home.

The catastrophe (shoah) which recently befell the Jewish people – the massacre of millions of Jews in Europe – was another clear demonstration of the urgency of solving the problem of its homelessness by re-establishing in Eretz-Israel the Jewish State, which would open the gates of the homeland wide to every Jew and confer upon the Jewish people the status of a fully privileged member of the community of nations.

Survivors of the Nazi holocaust in Europe, as well as Jews from other parts of the world, continued to migrate to Eretz-Israel, undaunted by difficulties, restrictions and dangers, and never ceased to assert their right to a life of dignity, freedom and honest toil in their national homeland.

In the Second World War, the Jewish community of this country contributed its full share to the struggle for the freedom of peace – loving nations against the forces of Nazi wickedness and, by the blood of its soldiers and its war effort, gained the right to be reckoned among the peoples who founded the United Nations.

On the 29th November, 1947, the United Nations General Assembly passed a resolution calling for the establishment of a Jewish State in Eretz-Israel; the General Assembly required the inhabitants of Eretz-Israel to take such steps as were necessary on their part for the implementation of that resolution. This recognition by the United Nations of the right of the Jewish people to establish their State is irrevocable.

This right is the natural right of the Jewish people to be masters of their own fate, like all other nations, in their own sovereign State.

ACCORDINGLY WE, MEMBERS OF THE PEOPLE'S COUNCIL, REPRESENTATIVES OF THE JEWISH COMMUNITY OF ERETZ-ISRAEL AND OF THE ZIONIST MOVEMENT, ARE HERE ASSEMBLED ON THE DAY OF THE TERMINATION OF THE BRITISH MANDATE OVER ERETZ-ISRAEL AND, BY VIRTUE OF OUR NATURAL AND HISTORIC RIGHT AND ON THE STRENGTH OF THE RESOLUTION OF THE UNITED NATIONS GENERAL ASSEMBLY, HEREBY DECLARE THE ESTABLISHMENT OF A JEWISH STATE IN ERETZ-ISRAEL, TO BE KNOWN AS THE STATE OF ISRAEL.

WE DECLARE that, with effect from the moment of the termination of the Mandate being tonight, the eve of Sabbath, the 6th Iyar, 5708 (14th May, 1948), until the establishment of the elected, regular authorities of the State in accordance with the Constitution which shall be adopted by the Elected Constituent Assembly not later than the 1st October 1948, the People's Council shall act as a Provisional Council of State, and its executive organ, the People's Administration, shall be the Provisional Government of the Jewish State, to be called "Israel".

THE STATE OF ISRAEL will be open for Jewish immigration and for the Ingathering of the Exiles; it will foster the development of the country for the benefit of all its inhabitants; it will be based on freedom, justice and peace as envisaged by the prophets of Israel; it will ensure complete equality of social and political rights to all its inhabitants irrespective of religion, race or sex; it will guarantee freedom of religion, conscience, language, education and culture; it will safeguard the Holy Places of all religions; and it will be faithful to the principles of the Charter of the United Nations.

THE STATE OF ISRAEL is prepared to cooperate with the agencies and representatives of the United Nations in implementing the resolution of the General Assembly of the 29th November, 1947, and will take steps to bring about the economic union of the whole of Eretz-Israel.

WE APPEAL to the United Nations to assist the Jewish people in the building-up of its State and to receive the State of Israel into the community of nations.

WE APPEAL – in the very midst of the onslaught launched against us now for months – to the Arab inhabitants of the State of Israel to preserve peace and participate in the upbuilding of the State on the basis of full and equal citizenship and due representation in all its provisional and permanent institutions.

WE EXTEND our hand to all neighbouring states and their peoples in an offer of peace and good neighbourliness, and appeal to them to establish bonds of cooperation and mutual help with the sovereign Jewish people settled in its own land. The State of Israel is prepared to do its share in a common effort for the advancement of the entire Middle East.

WE APPEAL to the Jewish people throughout the Diaspora to rally round the Jews of Eretz-Israel in the tasks of immigration and upbuilding and to stand by them in the great struggle for the realization of the age-old dream – the redemption of Israel.

PLACING OUR TRUST IN THE "ROCK OF ISRAEL", WE AFFIX OUR SIGNATURES TO THIS PROCLAMATION AT THIS SESSION OF THE PROVISIONAL COUNCIL OF STATE, ON THE SOIL OF THE HOMELAND, IN THE CITY OF TEL-AVIV, ON THIS SABBATH EVE, THE 5TH DAY OF IYAR, 5708 (14TH MAY, 1948).

Daniel Auster
Mordekhai Bentov
Yitzchak Ben Zvi
Eliyahu Berligne
Fritz Bernstein
Rabbi Wolf Gold
Meir Grabovsky
Yitzchak Gruenbaum
Dr Abraham Granovsky
Eliyahu Dobkin
Meir Wilner-Kovner
Zerach Wahrhaftig
Herzl Vardi
Rachel Cohen
Rabbi Kalman Kahana

Saadia Kobashi
Rabbi Yitzchak Meir Levin
Meir David Loewenstein
Zvi Luria
Golda Myerson
Nachum Nir
Zvi Segal
Rabbi Yehuda Leib Hacohen Fishman
David Zvi Pinkas
Aharon Zisling
Moshe Kolodny
Eliezer Kaplan
Abraham Katznelson

Felix Rosenblueth
David Remez
Berl Repetur
Mordekhai Shattner
Ben Zion Sternberg
Bekhor Shitreet
Moshe Shapira
Moshe Shertok[2]

---

2   Israel Ministry of Foreign Affairs, "The Declaration of the Establishment of the State of Israel", 14 May 1948.

And with that, the entire assembly stood to sing the Hatikvah, the Israeli national anthem.

Later that night the United States became the first country to recognize the newly formed State of Israel. However, Egypt, Trans-Jordan, Iraq, and Syria launched an attack on Israel which started the Arab–Israeli war; a war that has been ongoing in varying levels of intensity ever since.

This begs the question: did God make a mistake in bringing the Jewish people back to the land at this time? We will consider the story of the Israeli Arab and Palestinian people later in this book.

But first, we will stay with recounting the rebirth of the nation of Israel and tell the story of one man who lived during this time. His name was Zvi Kalisher.

Zvi Kalisher's story

Born Henryk (Zvi in Hebrew) Weichert Kalisher, Zvi was born into a Jewish family in Poland and, although he survived the Holocaust, he lost his entire family. When Germany invaded Poland in 1939, Zvi was eleven years old. His mother, in a desperate bid to save his life, took him to an orphanage to be cared for; she reasoned that with his fair hair and blue eyes nobody would guess he was Jewish. Her parting words to her son were, "Be strong and never tell anyone that you are a Jew. From now on you are a man!"

Zvi learned to speak German in the orphanage and was later taken to Berlin to join the Hitler youth. However, due to his small stature, he was considered unsuitable and duly returned to Poland. This gave him the opportunity to search for his family. But by this time, Polish Jews had been arrested and sent to the Warsaw ghetto. Zvi went in search of them. The story of the horrors he encountered there – starvation, brutality, desperation, death, and disease – are told in his book, *Zvi: The Miraculous Story of Triumph over the Holocaust* by Elwood

McQuaid.[3] He never did find his parents and, after surviving by living off his wits, scrounging for food, and living by hiding in the forests, by the time the war was over, aged seventeen, Zvi made his way to Israel when it was still known as British Mandate Palestine. After Israel's independence was declared on 14 May 1948, he was drafted into the Israeli army to fight in the war with the Arab nations that began immediately after that date. Still weakened from his experience of surviving the Second World War and with no time to recover, there would be no respite for Zvi.

In November 2017, I met Zvi's son, Victor Kalisher. He told me how his father, having survived against all the odds, questioned why God had spared his life. It was soon after coming to Israel and having fought in the Arab/Israeli war of independence, that he became a believer in Yeshua and met his wife. They, together with their four children became one of the first Messianic Jewish families in Israel. Today, Victor is the Director of Bible Society work in Israel and later in this book, when we ask the question, "What is a Messianic Jew?" we will explore his story.

But first we must discover more about the early days of the rebirth of the nation of Israel. How did it happen? With so many hostile nations surrounding Israel intent on her destruction, and with a people who had been traumatized from the Holocaust, what sort of a future could they hope for?

In the next chapter, we will take inspiration from the story of Tel Aviv. Today, it is a vibrant city. But just over one hundred years ago, the area that is now Tel Aviv, lying just to the north of the ancient biblical port of Jaffa, was mile after mile of sand dunes!

---

3   Elwood McQuaid, *Zvi: The Miraculous Story of Triumph over the Holocaust*, (Westville NJ: Friends of Israel Gospel Ministry, 2000.)

9

THE STORY OF TEL AVIV

This city perfectly demonstrates the optimism and energy that Jewish people are blessed with. To visit Tel Aviv today is to visit a vibrant, modern city that is home to over four million Jewish people. Situated just north of the ancient port of Jaffa (also known as Joppa), the biblical city made famous by Jonah and the whale, and by Peter who visited the home of Simon the Tanner, Tel Aviv lies on the eastern shores of the Mediterranean Sea. With sandy beaches stretching from Gaza in the south to Haifa in the north, an idyllic position, and a warm climate, Tel Aviv became the obvious place to build a new city. Today, looking across Tel Aviv from the top of one of the many tall buildings that stand as a monument to the pioneering spirit of those early settlers, it is hard to imagine that just over one hundred years ago, none of this existed. Instead, we would have seen mile after mile of sand dunes stretching far into the north.

But as Jewish immigration increased at the turn of the twentieth century, Jaffa became overcrowded. This port city was then largely occupied by Arabs and, understandably, with overcrowding came tension and so a solution had to be found.

On 11 April 1909, sixty-six Jewish families arranged to meet at a spot on the sand dunes to the north of Jaffa. They had decided it was time to move out of the overcrowded city of Jaffa and build a new neighbourhood. They were planning to call it Ahuzat Bayit, meaning "homestead". Indeed that was its name for a while until, that is, Tel Aviv was chosen in 1910. Tel Aviv means, "hill of spring" and a verse in Ezekiel inspired the name: "Then I came to the colony of Judean exiles in Tel-abib, beside the Kebar River." (Ezekiel 3:15)

It was felt that this verse inspired the dream of a restored Jewish nation. The word "tel" means an ancient mound comprised of layers of previous settlements, while "aviv" is the Hebrew word for "spring", suggesting renewal.

It was time for each family to be allocated a plot of land. But how could this be done fairly in a way that didn't show favouritism? The idea for a lottery was mentioned and agreed. Akiva Arieh Weiss, the chairman of the group of families, then walked along the beach and collected sixty-six grey sea shells and sixty-six white sea shells. He wrote the names of each family on the white sea shells and the plot numbers on the grey shells. It was then a simple matter to draw a white sea shell out of the bag and then a grey sea shell and pair them together to provide each family with their own plot of land on which they could start to plan their home and begin building the first modern Hebrew city!

Almost thirty years later, during the 1930s, Jewish immigration to Israel began to increase rapidly as Jews were fleeing Europe as anti-Semitism and persecution spread like gathering storm clouds. The population of Tel Aviv grew very quickly and, by 1936, 130,000 people lived there.

If Jerusalem is the conservative, religious capital of Israel, then Tel Aviv is the secular, commercial city. It is a Jewish city. By contrast, neighbouring Jaffa is largely, but not exclusively, Arab.

But we are looking at modern Israel and trying to understand what God is doing there today and so we will look at Tel Aviv through the eyes and experience of believers who live there now, beginning with Avi Mizrachi.

Avi Mizrachi's story

In April 2017, I met Avi on the twelfth floor of an office block in downtown Tel Aviv in a room he called the "Prayer Tower" and we stood by the windows and looked out over Tel Aviv. To our left lay the blue sea of the Mediterranean. To the south lay Jaffa. To the north and east, stretching as far as the eye could see, lay modern Tel Aviv; a mixture of tall modern blocks of offices and apartments, many with balconies, and original buildings which almost seemed dwarfed by their more modern counterparts. Avi told me a bit more about the first settlers to Tel Aviv:

These were mainly Jewish families who had left Russia and Eastern Europe because of the pogroms and the persecution of the early 1900s and they came to the port of Jaffa during the Turkish Ottoman period. Their dream was to build a beautiful city on the sand dunes, a Jewish city where Hebrew would be spoken. Education, in Hebrew, was high on their list of priorities and in 1909 they moved the Herzliya Gymnasium school, which had started in Jaffa in 1905, to Tel Aviv.

Today approximately 3 million Jewish people live in the Tel Aviv area. Tel Aviv has always been known as a centre for commerce, banking, business, culture, and tourism. And there is plenty of nightlife too – Tel Aviv is known as the city that never stops! During the day it's alive with business and commerce, but at night it comes alive in a different way!

Avi Mizrachi is the pastor of an Israeli Messianic congregation in downtown Tel Aviv–Jaffa and he is an enthusiastic evangelist; his heart is to tell people about Yeshua. Is he encouraged?

It's going very well. We believe in prayer. Everything starts in prayer. Five years ago, when I was in a conference in Korea, the Lord spoke to me and said I should build an altar of prayer and worship and pray for breakthrough in this my city of Tel Aviv. So we opened this House of Prayer in this room where we are standing now. We invited all the pastors and leaders of congregations, both here in Tel Aviv and beyond the city, to the opening. They all came and we dedicated the place to the Lord. I gave each pastor a key to the door and told them this is your place too. Several different groups come on a weekly basis to pray for breakthrough in the city. I am praying that before long there will be 100 congregations in Tel Aviv alone because the harvest is ready. People here are very secular yet they are very open to the gospel.

Tel Aviv is known as a city of young people. While there are some families who live in the heart of the city, most families live in the suburbs and commute into Tel Aviv to work. Apartments have become very expensive. The gay movement is very strong here; Tel Aviv is very secular. When we talk to people on the streets they say, "If you want to talk about God, then go to Jerusalem!" We tell them that we are not religious, we just love the Lord. We give them an alternative; we tell them, "You can know God: you can know the Lord without becoming a religious Orthodox Jew." When we present the gospel in a very simple way and tell people that God loves them and he sent the Messiah, Yeshua, to atone for their sin they are shocked because they've never heard that before. As a result, we find they are very open to listen. The harvest in Tel Aviv is ready.

"Is God doing something here that will impact the nations of the world?" I asked Avi.

The gospel has gone out from Jerusalem to the ends of the earth, just as Jesus said. Now we see the gospel coming back home to Jerusalem, having gone right around the earth. I believe that as we are entering the end times, we will see a large revival coming to Israel. The veil will be removed from the Jewish people's eyes and they will see who the Messiah is. As Scripture says, when this happens, "It will be life for those who were dead!" (Romans 11:15).

I believe we are living in the end times and if we want to see the King of Kings and Lord of Lords coming back to Jerusalem, we have to pray and work hard for all Israel to be saved, because that is what is on God's agenda.

Tel Aviv is a vibrant city where many are successful. But not everybody who finds their way here has a positive experience. Alongside the wealthy banking and commercial areas, there are districts where many poor people live, some of them are homeless and addicted to drugs and alcohol. For these people, newly arrived in what they were hoping would be a safe haven after suffering years of persecution and anti-Semitism, to find themselves without hope and full of regrets can be a burden too hard to bear.

Through the story of Tel Aviv and some of the people who live there, we have now caught a glimpse of modern Israel, a country that has risen out of the ashes. In less than one hundred years, since declaring independence in 1948, Israel has taken its place on the world stage. Israel has shown this is a country capable of holding its own, defending itself against enemies from both outside and within, educating its people, leading the world in technology, medicine, and science. However, it has also been a nation that has had to fight endless battles while, at the same time, welcoming and providing homes for the thousands of Jews who have made Aliyah from the nations they once called home but which no longer feel safe.

But this book is about understanding modern Israel from God's perspective. Yes, we have considered how many thousands of Jewish people have and are returning to live there just as the Scriptures foretold. It's their stories that we will now focus on against the backdrop of the political unrest and tensions, wars and threats of wars. And of course, Israel is not just home to Jewish people: Arabs live there too. So what about their stories? Where do they fit into God's plans?

We will now consider what life has been like in Israel since 1948 until the present day through the stories of the people themselves.

10

SINCE 1948 – WARS AND ALIYAH

Why has it happened that one of the smallest nations of the world, with one of the smallest populations, has been constantly at the centre of world news and opinion for its entire existence? In fact, the reality is even worse because, as we have already discussed in this book, throughout its entire history, from earliest days, Israel and the Jewish people have seldom enjoyed a prolonged period of peace and security.

However, this is not a history book! Rather we are attempting to understand modern Israel through the lens of the Bible and the stories of people who live there today, people who are believers, both Jews and Arabs.

Since 1948, when modern Israel was reborn, there have been wars. Neighbouring Arab nations have attacked on numerous occasions. Today, Iran is issuing dire threats against Israel. Israel's immediate neighbours – Lebanon, Syria, Jordan, and Egypt – have housed (and still do) militant groups that threaten Israel's existence frequently.

You may wonder why anybody would choose to leave a nation where their family has lived for generations, albeit not always safely, to go and live in Israel – a place that is constantly being threatened and where everybody from the age of eighteen is expected to join the defence force!

The facts show that, despite the challenges, people have flocked back to Israel and are still returning. People like Israel Pochtar.

Israel Pochtar's story – from the Crimea to Israel

I first met Israel in September 2019 in Ashdod, where he now lives and works along with his wife and family. Ashdod is very close to Gaza and subject to rocket attacks when unrest on the Gaza/Israel border flares up from time to time. This ancient biblical city, like Tel Aviv, is situated on the coastline. In fact, the beachfront is beautiful, just like in Tel Aviv. Today, alongside the ancient lies the new city of Ashdod. It is a building site! There are cranes everywhere and apartment blocks are springing up across the skyline to house new immigrants. There is a large port at Ashdod, the entry point for goods coming into the country and for goods being exported from Israel around the world.

I had heard that Israel Pochtar had moved to Ashdod from Tel Aviv to start a new congregation there a few years ago. It is called Beit Hallel – House of Praise. I had been following this story because not only had the congregation grown quickly, it had also been subject to some serious persecution from religious Orthodox Jews who clearly considered this congregation a threat to Judaism.

We met in the building where the congregation meets at present. Next door, there is a newer, much bigger building and, when we visited in September 2019, the first floor of this building was being adapted for the Beit Hallel congregation to move into. And the reason for the move? The existing space is now too small for this fast-growing congregation.

Israel Pochtar's story is a good example of what God is doing in bringing Jewish people from the nations to live in Israel. And all this is happening in a climate of ongoing wars, political tension and economic challenge. The cost of living in Israel is high. To come with nothing, have to learn the language, find a home and establish yourself takes time, determination and faith.

I was born into a Jewish family in Crimea. My family were secular but we knew we were Jewish. When I was growing up I had many conversations about God but not with my parents, rather with my great grandma; she was the one who taught me about God and our Jewish heritage. I came to live in Israel when I was twenty-two years old. My parents had passed away. I came with my wife and our new baby."

"Why did you come?" I asked Israel Pochtar.

I believed God was leading me, talking to me. I was reading the Bible and I found out more and more about God's plan for the people of Israel and I understood that part of his plan was to bring them back to the land of Israel. This touched me a lot and I had been praying about it and had the feeling that maybe one day when I had grown older and retired, then I would move to accomplish the Word of God! But by the age of twenty-one, I just knew that I was to go to Israel not sometime in the future but now.

"When you came to Israel with your wife and baby, where did you first live?"

We landed in Tel Aviv and we stayed there for the first ten years of our life in Israel. It was a blessing to be in a place that was open to ideas, not necessarily about Jesus and faith in Yeshua, but a place that was open to all sorts of different people.

"When you arrived, did you have to find a job? How did you get started?"

Like many of the families who make Aliyah, we didn't have any close relatives here and the government provided us with accommodation for a few days in a simple hotel in Tel Aviv. We stayed there until we found an apartment we could rent.

Understanding Modern Israel

"Were those early days difficult for you?"

Yes, it was difficult but, praise God, we were young! When you're young, it's easier to adapt to all the changes and challenges you're exposed to. We felt God was leading us and we were stepping forward by faith. After we had found an apartment, the next day I found a job; I was working in construction for a few years. Within a couple of weeks we had found a congregation because back then in the mid 1990s, congregations were almost underground. They weren't officially underground, but they acted like an underground church. We had no internet then so we couldn't Google! But by a miracle we found a congregation almost immediately. There was a young Russian-speaking Messianic congregation in Tel Aviv and one day they made an announcement in the local newspaper. It was the first and last time they did this because newspapers did not allow Christians or Messianic believers to publish articles. But somehow the editors didn't understand that this was about faith in Jesus and they let them make an announcement the same week we arrived! So as I opened the newspaper looking for jobs, I found the announcement and I found believers!

"You started with a Russian-speaking congregation because presumably at that time you were having to learn Hebrew?"

Well we went to this congregation and they helped us to find the congregation we needed and two weeks after that we joined the Beit Emmanuel congregation, one of the congregations in Tel Aviv that is Hebrew-speaking. There we met a family who had arrived a couple of years before us, and they provided translation for us because, yes, we needed to learn Hebrew!

"As you mentioned, in the mid-1990s the number of Messianic believers in the land was very small."

Yes indeed, statistically as I remember there were just a couple of thousand people; the Body of Messiah was very small then.

"You worked in the construction industry, but when did you realize that God had another job for you?"

During the first few months of being in Israel God called me to share the gospel and work for the kingdom here in the land. The first challenge was age – I was very young; then language and culture. But I knew God had called me and I knew that I was not just going to have a "normal" job, rather I knew he was preparing a place for me.

After a couple of years working in construction, my Israeli pastor offered me the opportunity to be an evangelist in the congregation. Beit Emmanuel then was a small congregation and the biggest need in a small congregation is for people. So I was hired to work for the congregation with a focus on evangelism to share the gospel with the people of Israel. It was a pretty quick journey!

I went to the streets, the parks, the beach – anywhere where people gathered, I went to speak with them. It was difficult, it was tough. Not many people responded. But I was happy because I knew, by the inspiration of the Holy Spirit, we needed to press on and share the gospel and trust the Lord that eventually he would bring about change and touch hearts.

"You say it was tough; today people seem more open. Describe the mindset of the people you were talking to. Why was it tough?"

It was difficult for a few reasons. One of the biblical reasons is where it says in the Scriptures that the veil of Moses is covering the eyes of the Jewish people and they cannot see. But in the same Scripture it also says that when they turn to God then Yeshua, Jesus, will take the veil from their eyes. So first of all it's a spiritual blindness as described prophetically in the Bible both in the Old and New Testaments. But God has promised that one day he will open the eyes of the Jewish people.

Secondly, I can understand the depth of rejection by the Jewish people because many of the people I was encountering then were survivors of the Second World War and the Holocaust. People who ran from the Second World War and the Nazis, who came here to Israel, in their view, in their mindset, they saw German Nazi soldiers as Christians because they wore crosses and some of them went to church. So they saw those German soldiers as people who were killing our nation and killing us. In addition, we have the history of Jewish persecution throughout church history; church history is not on our side. I hear many Christians today say, "But we are different." And yes, that is right, but in the eyes of Jewish people the Inquisitions were caused by Christian people, and the Nazis were Christians. Over the centuries, history tells us that often Christians did persecute Jewish people. We know that is not "real" Christianity, it's not biblical Christianity, but again in the perception of Jewish people they see what Christians have done to us. The Bible tells us that love overcomes. It takes time to explain to people. It takes time to work through all these barriers and prejudices. But praise the Lord for the Holy Spirit; here and there he would touch people and open their hearts to give them understanding and revelation that it's not real Christians or Jesus who were behind these persecutions, rather it's bad history – but there is hope in Jesus. It's a long process, but little by little over a couple of decades I have seen lots and lots of changes.

"Let's follow your story: you became involved with the Beit Emmanuel congregation in Jaffa, but now you're in Ashdod, so what happened?"

Well, I had a supernatural encounter with God. It happened after I'd been living ten years in Tel Aviv. The congregation had grown and we were experiencing a time of revival. We saw many people come to faith. I was happy doing what I was doing. I was young, an associate pastor and street evangelist, building the congregation and seeing the kingdom of God coming. It was a wonderful time. But right in the middle of this happy and fulfilling time, I went to Ashdod to visit a family. I had led them to the Lord and now I was on my way to visit them. I was driving my car and while praying in the Spirit, I had a supernatural experience with God. Everything around me disappeared and I saw a vision. I saw a big congregation with many Israelis worshipping Yeshua. I saw a Bible school and youth conferences, people coming from the nations, lots of details. But the main emphasis was the large local congregation that was very active. By the end of the vision I heard a voice. I don't know whether it was a physical voice or an inner voice; but it was loud and clear and said, "Leave everything behind, move to Ashdod and start this congregation."

Well, that changed my life! I came home and shared with my family, my pastor, and my friends that God had spoken to me about leaving Tel Aviv and moving to Ashdod to start the first Hebrew-speaking congregation in the city.

"Were there other congregations here at that time?"

There was a French congregation that no longer exists, and a Russian-speaking congregation, but no Hebrew-speaking congregation. And the vision I had seen was specifically about a Hebrew-speaking congregation for Israelis. In a city of 250,000, there was no Hebrew-speaking congregation at that time and 75 per cent of the people spoke Hebrew only. So obviously there was a need.

"What did you wife say when you told her you were moving to Ashdod?"

Well at first she just cried! She didn't like the idea. Young families love Tel Aviv. We had two little kids and we had many friends and lots of activities. Ashdod is a pleasant city to live in today, but back then, there was a big difference between Ashdod and Tel Aviv. So she just cried, but after a few days of prayer, she came to the point where she recognized God had spoken and through her tears she said, "Yes Lord!"

"How do you go about starting a new work in a city like this?"

I started to come to Ashdod once a week to pray. There is a place called Jonah Hill – it's the highest natural point in Ashdod. So I would go to Jonah Hill to pray over the city. I would pray for the city and God started to send people from different nations, from England, from Switzerland, from America, and they said, "We heard about your vision and we want to come and pray for you." So I started to come more often, two or three times a week with new friends, different people who would support the vision God gave me. We had a year of preparation in the Spirit – I knew I would be moving to Ashdod within a year of having had the vision. Six months into this time of preparation, I started a home group with some people God brought to me. They were people who were planning to move to Ashdod. We studied the Bible together and prayed. Prayer, prayer, prayer… lots of prayers.

"A big vision but only a few people to begin with. Were you ever tempted to give up? Did you even wonder, is this really God?"

No, I never had this temptation because the vision I received was so strong, so clear and obvious. Looking back now, thinking about the early steps, the persecution we faced, the challenges and difficulties, the option of giving up was never an option because of the vision God gave me.

"It is interesting that God had spoken independently to other people and encouraged them to join you."

Yes, that was very encouraging because seeking the Lord and praying at the beginning, the start of the congregation, I had many questions to God. I had seen a vision – but that was the final destination! I didn't know all the details and the process of what God was going to do. But in the process of us starting the congregation and having devotional times with the Lord, God started to talk with me about other congregations that we were going to plant from Ashdod! And it shocked me! I then had even more questions to God! "How am I going to do that?" You're a young leader only thirty years old! We need people to start these congregations. We need money. But God has been very gracious to speak to my concerns and giving me words of encouragement basically saying he would give me all the resources I would need. "When you need wisdom, I will give you wisdom. When you need the power of God, you will have power. When you need joy, you will receive joy. When you need people to accomplish vision, I will send you people." God has been faithful through all these years and I've seen people being added and supernaturally moved to Ashdod to come and help with the ministry and people rising up from within the congregation – getting saved, growing in the Lord, and becoming leaders, fulfilling the vision.

"Perhaps we could talk about Ashdod. Today it's a new city. Biblically, there's been an Ashdod for centuries. Just describe what day-to-day life is like here in this city."

Ashdod is ancient and modern. It is a biblical city and there are prophecies in the Bible about Ashdod. Modern Ashdod is fifty-seven years old with tall buildings, situated on the coast with beautiful beaches. The majority of Israelis living here are eastern Israelis; Jews who came from Muslim countries such as Yemen and Morocco. There is also a large Russian Jewish population here of approximately 50,000 Israelis, from Georgia, Armenia, Ukraine, Bella Russia, and other countries from the former Soviet Union. There are also many French Jews and Jews from Ethiopia. There is a large port here where many people work. And because Ashdod is relatively close to Tel Aviv, we have people in the congregation who work there in IT and high tech businesses. The community in Ashdod is not as secular as Tel Aviv; most of the people here are very family orientated and practice a traditional form of Judaism. We also have a large and growing religious Orthodox community as well.

"You are also very close to Gaza: has that had an enormous impact on life here?"

Yes, it is a factor in our city because from time to time we have rockets from Gaza landing here. Usually we are warned when the threat of attacks are likely. Two years ago, the situation was very tough when we had fifty days of fire and Ashdod was hit by 300 missiles. Ninety per cent of them were intercepted but even so we could see rocket fire and explosions in the sky and thirty rockets landed in the city. It was a stressful time as every time the siren went off we had to run to bomb shelters. For families with young children, this was particularly difficult. Schools and kindergartens were closed during this time because it was too dangerous to have them open.

But normally, Ashdod is a beautiful, safe city with very little crime. It is safe to wander around the city after dark. It's a great city to raise a family. So there are lots of families with young children here. For example, in our congregation of Beit Hallel, we have about 200 adults and more than 100 kids. So we're a very young and vibrant congregation.

"Let's talk about how the congregation grew. You mentioned there are a lot of prophetic words in the Bible to do with

Ashdod, so maybe we could talk a little bit about that and how that has encouraged you as well."

Yes, when I knew we were moving to Ashdod, I studied the Bible to find all the Scriptures that mentioned Ashdod and I discovered verses I hadn't seen in the Bible before! For example in Zechariah 9:6–7 (I checked translations and discovered the NIV was the most accurate) it says the Philistines will be destroyed (and that happened even before the time of Jesus) but that those who are left (speaking about the last days) will belong to our God and will become leaders in Judah. So that inspired me a lot because here we see two clear promises, first of all the city will belong to our God (which is revival in the city); and, second, we will be leaders in Judah (that encouraged me to think about any influence God would give us outside of Ashdod and we began to plant other congregations in other places). It's amazing to find your city in the Bible, to read the prophecies and literally see them fulfilled. In Amos 3, it says, "Proclaim from the [rooftops] of Ashdod." Our new church building has a rooftop!

"When you share this with people in your congregation, are they as excited about it as you are or are they just surviving and busy leading their own lives?"

It's both! Sometimes we have to remind ourselves about these prophecies because, yes, when you're living your daily life and daily routine, daily challenges and raising kids, you can forget these verses!

"There are some famous stories in the Bible about things that happened in Ashdod – some of them were quite terrible."

Yes, there were some terrible destructions because when you read in the Bible about the Assyrian and Babylonian, Greek, and Roman empires, they all came through Israel and the city of Ashdod was destroyed again and again along with Ashkelon, Gaza, and Jerusalem. Also Ashdod has seen judgments of God involving the Philistines. When the Israelites lost the Ark of the Covenant the first time, the Philistines took it and brought it to Ashdod, to the Temple of Dagon. And that was when the heavy hand of the Lord was on the Philistines and they suffered from epidemics, the statue of Dagon fell in the temple and its head and arms broke off. So the presence of God was here with the Ark of the Covenant, but not for good because it was a wrong thing to have brought it here. In the New Testament, we read the story of Philip the evangelist – after he preached the gospel to the Ethiopian eunuch, he later arrived in Ashdod (in some Bibles this is called Azotus in Acts 8, but in Hebrew the name is Ashdod).

"Let's return to the story of how your congregation grew. You started off as a house church with your family and a few others. You grew to thirty people and the congregation was launched. What's happened since then?"

Many things have happened since then! We've always been very active in evangelism; it's central to everything we do. God has also encouraged us to take care of the poor and needy and help new immigrants and Holocaust survivors so that we have become a hub of help for many people. But whatever we do, we are always evangelizing and sharing the gospel and not allowing the busyness of life to distract us from the main reason why we're here which is to preach the gospel. It's wonderful to take care of the poor and needy and we do that in a big way – but preaching the gospel is the heart of who we are, along with raising young leaders and investing our time in the young generation of Israelis, to inspire them to walk in the power of God and see the transformation of society in Israel.

We have, and still do, suffer from persecution. We work within certain legal limitations; we know the law and we work within it. We see revival is coming, changes are here and, as a pastor, I'm really encouraged.

"You say you have legal challenges and one of those challenges is that you cannot evangelize young people under the age of eighteen and you mention you have experienced persecution, so you're up against it on at least a couple of fronts."

Yes, we had a thousand religious Orthodox people led by rabbis who came to the doors of the congregation to speak against us on the media using the TV, radio channels, and newspapers. They did this for years. We had small groups of Orthodox people coming to every Shabbat meeting. They would stand at the doors screaming and shouting, trying to scare people out. They vowed to close our congregation years ago. But they haven't succeeded and we have grown 300 per cent since that started and we keep growing! Recently they have given up persecutions of this kind as they realize it doesn't help. A picture of me and my wife was printed on a poster and put on the walls of the city along with my home address and later my assistants and their wives had the same treatment. We've been followed in our cars by Orthodox people, watching us. They have written many negative articles about us in newspapers with Nazi images alongside us. But in the midst of all this pressure, the congregation kept growing – nothing could stop us because God was working through us and was with us. It was God's grace that helped and protected us.

"That level of intimidation is very unpleasant. Were you ever physically in danger?"

No. I've been spat at. I've been followed and cursed, sometimes in front of my kids, by Orthodox leaders. They shouted spiritual curses at us. But God has promised us his joy when we face persecution for the sake of the Lord and that's my experience. It was difficult. I cannot say it wasn't tough. Yet, through all these years we have experienced such an amazing presence of God and encouragement of the Holy Spirit so to give up was never an option. The Holy Spirit renewed his love and power in us every day. It's not because I'm strong that we've been able to continue. Rather it's the grace of God working in us and through us. I've had experiences of fear and intimidation and uncertainty, but I can say in the midst of difficult days, we would come to pray and when we feel pressure like a storm coming against us, I would close my eyes and the presence of the Lord was enormous. So then joy comes and love comes and power to forgive these people and pray for our persecutors. So it's amazing to see how God's kingdom works. Even when you think you're not prepared, the Holy Spirit is always with us, lifting us up, and making us stronger.

"Would it be true to say that the spirit of hatred and anger that has been shown through these people persecuting you is very much the same spirit that the Pharisees and Sadducees showed against Jesus?"

Yes, exactly. That's what we really feel and see – the same spirit of anti-Christ that was released through people who rejected Jesus in this land. Jewish people were first to receive him and Jewish people were first to reject him. It's like a family business; we're dealing with the same protesters, those Orthodox who try to stop what we do and stop growth and the message of Jesus. Yet many Israelis come to hear and listen and check things out for themselves and then come to know the Lord.

"What is God doing in Israel? You're involved with other pastors here in Israel, both Messianic and Arab pastors. How would you answer that question?"

First of all, there are many changes taking place in Israel – "kingdom" changes. The population of Israel is growing, the economy is strong, and the challenges are also growing. It's definitely a blessed nation but it's not an easy nation to live in. But the most exciting thing for me as a pastor is to see what God is doing. And God is really on the move. I cannot say revival has come yet, but the changes are enormous. We see how the young people are searching for answers. They get tired of the conflict. They wonder what the future is for Palestinians and Israelis. There does not seem to be any political way to resolve the conflict; many people have tried but nothing has worked. But we know the promises of God and he promised that the prophecy in Isaiah 19 will happen when Jewish people will worship the God of Israel together with Arab nations in Jerusalem. This gives us a reason to believe there will be a major revival in all the countries of the Middle East in Israel along with Israeli Arabs, Palestinians, and Jewish people. We are reaching the point where we see Jesus is the only way, the Bible is the only hope, biblical prophecy is our only hope. I would say to people who do not care about the Jewish people and Israel, it matters to God! It's written in the Bible and what God has promised will never change. And God promised in the Old and New Testaments that "all Israel will be saved". The gospel was first preached to a group of Jewish people who then went to the nations and they changed the nations with the gospel. Now it's time for the nations to come and bring the gospel back to Israel and join hands to help with revival in the land.

"What are you expecting to see, hear, and witness in the next two to three years?"

We expect to see more of the favour of God, change in society in general, and of course salvation. Now speaking of salvation, it's been a slow growth, but we are expecting to see that speed up.

"You're describing a situation where people are much bolder than they were thirty years ago, they're very much more willing to talk about their faith. Can you tell me a little about the Arab people and Muslims who are coming to faith?"

To work with Muslims in Israel and the West Bank is very, very difficult. So mostly this work is underground. We hear that God is moving in Muslim areas but it is difficult to keep track of it because many times they cannot speak openly. It's hard to believe that only a few miles away (in Gaza) people are living a completely different life. But we hear from Arab pastors how many are coming to the Lord.

"I am hearing reports of young people who are believers going abroad as missionaries from Israel to other nations. Is that part of your experience here?"

Yes, I have a number of young people who, when they got saved, had a passion to travel to the nations to share their faith. They are receiving a supernatural love for other nations. One young man in our congregation went to Norway where he met a Syrian refugee and he was saved. They are working as evangelists together in the Norwegian church – Jew and Arab!

Israel Pochtar ended by talking about how this Jew and Arab are working together as evangelists. So what about the Arab people living in Israel, and the Palestinian Arab people living in Gaza and the West Bank? Where do they fit into the story of modern Israel and what God is doing there today? We now turn our attention to some of their stories and begin to see how unexpected things are happening that may feel counter-intuitive to us.

11

WHAT ABOUT THE ARABS?

We're going to start with a story in the present and work backwards! The story is about a man called Hanna Eid.

Hanna Eid's story

Hanna is an Israeli Arab, married to Lena, who is also an Israeli Arab. He was born in Eilaboun, she was born in Cana – both Arab towns in northern Israel. Cana is well known as being the place where Jesus turned water into wine.

Why tell their story in the context of this book? Because it is a story that perfectly demonstrates how God is working among sections of the Christian Israeli Arab population in northern Israel, overturning the hatred, bitterness, distrust, and even betrayal that occurred in 1948 during the Arab–Israeli war when thousands of Arabs were made to leave their villages by the Israeli army "for security reasons". Many never returned. Others did return and, today, there are scores of Arab villages in northern Israel where the overwhelming majority are Muslim; and a few are Christian. However, after all these years, and despite the ongoing hostilities and disagreements between Arabs and Jews within Israel (we will consider the Palestinian situation in the West Bank and Gaza separately), what has recently slowly but surely emerged are a significant number of Christian Israeli Arabs who are prepared to not only forgive those responsible for events of the past, but who are actively seeking to come together and build bridges with Messianic Jewish believers in a spirit of reconciliation and forgiveness.

In September 2019, I visited Eilaboun, a village in northern Israel situated close to the Sea of Galilee, a short distance north of Tiberias. (The story of what happened there in 1948 will be described at the end of this chapter). I had met Hanna Eid and his wife Lena the year before – they live in Eilaboun and Hanna is the pastor of an evangelical church there. Having heard from a number of Israeli Arabs whose families fled their villages in 1948, Eilaboun being one of them, I was keen to visit the village and hear the story of what happened there but to also witness what is happening there today. Hanna had kindly agreed to be my guide for the day.

After lunch at their house, we went up onto the flat roof. Eilaboun is situated on a hill top and as we looked at the hills all around us, Hanna described what we were looking at.

We are here on our rooftop in Eilaboun and in the distance we can see a number of Arab villages that God has opened the doors for us to visit. In the distance you can see Maghar. Maghar is mainly a Druze town; about 23,000 people live there. God has opened the doors for a women's ministry and it's amazing how God is healing the hearts of the women there. My wife, Lena, tells me often that she meets women there who have heavy, sad hearts but the message of Christ is healing them. The women meet together every two weeks and currently over thirty women come to this meeting.

The other place we can see is Deir Hanna. In 2010, God opened the door for us to start a home group there and it's still going, every other Friday. There are no evangelical churches in Deir Hanna and our vision and our hope is that we will eventually have a church there to speak about Christ.

Further to the west, just out of view, is another town God has opened the door for us. It's called Sakhnin and we have several couples from there who come to our church here in Eilaboun.

Many years ago, God put these towns in my heart and I believe God is calling me and my wife to start ministry in these towns with the church here in Eilaboun being, as it were, the mother church. We know that God has called us to work amongst the Arab people here in the Galilee area.

Hanna had earlier told me that he was born in Eilaboun. He studied civil engineering at the Technion University in Haifa, and I was interested to know why he had decided to return and become a pastor when he could have been enjoying a more prosperous lifestyle elsewhere.

Yes, I was born here and my father was born here. He was born in 1911, before the establishment of the State of Israel. At first, I thought God was calling me to some of the surrounding places, but a few years ago it became very clear that God was calling me to my home town of Eilaboun. My wife and I have a heart for our people. We work with women, with children, and with couples – and God is glorifying his name in the Galilee. I remember when Jesus was walking through the Galilee preaching and proclaiming the good news and we feel we are carrying on his work in taking the gospel into this area to people that need a lot of hope. We feel that Christians in the West do not know about us Arab believers living here in northern Israel. But the Galilee is full of Arabs! And I believe that this place is very precious to our Lord's heart. I know that God has put us in this place.

We started our walk around Eilaboun. It was a very hot afternoon. We met few people. There was no traffic. It was very quiet. As we walked along the road, Hanna described that Eilaboun is unusual because it is not a Muslim village. The majority of the inhabitants today are nominal Christians, he told me:

Approximately 6,000 people live here and 70 per cent of them are Catholic. I am taking you to meet my elderly sister. While we had the same father, my sister's mother (his first wife) died and he remarried my mother who was much younger. When I was born, I was quite literally the baby of the family!

One day, an evangelical minister came to our village and visited my sister's house. He was helping her son who is blind. But it's an amazing story of how, through this blind boy, the work in Eilaboun began.

After walking for a few minutes, we came to a house and Hanna stopped outside.

Here it is – my sister's home. This is where the home group started. You can see the cross above the door here. This became the first evangelical church in Eilaboun. I was married here in 2002! But let's go inside and meet the people here, in the room where the home group started.

As we walked into the house, an elderly lady came to greet us. She was indeed much older than Hanna. We were introduced:

This is my sister, Wedad, and her husband, Radee. They are the ones who started the ministry here in Eilaboun. Still they come to our church and they are a great blessing. I will ask my sister to tell us a little about the start of the church here.

And speaking in Arabic to his sister then translating into English, his sister's story unfolded.

I will tell you what happened to me. In 1973 our son George had an accident and injured his eyes. The doctor told us that he needed surgery but there was only a 1 per cent chance of success. However, I agreed and signed for the surgery and I told the Lord I believed he could heal my son. I promised the Lord that if he healed George, I would believe in him. God healed George; his sight was restored. We returned home, but I soon forgot the promise I had made to the Lord.

Eighteen months later, the problem came back and George's eyesight deteriorated. I turned again to the Lord and told him I believed he could heal him. I admitted that I had lied the first time, but I promised that this time I would believe in the Lord and turn to him if he healed my son. For the second time, the surgery went well and God healed his eyes and George's sight was restored. After nearly three months in hospital, he returned home and everything was alright.

But again, I forgot about my promise to the Lord. Two years later, the problem returned to George's eyes and the pain in his head was severe. He was sixteen years old. I prayed to the Lord and admitted that I had lied twice and doubted whether he would listen to my prayers again."

By this time, Wedad was weeping bitterly.

When he returned from the hospital, a minister from the town of Tur'an, who knew about us, came and offered to help us and read the Bible to George. He encouraged me to sit with them and listen to the words he was reading. In those days, I was part of the Catholic church and this man was an evangelical so I was not sure about him and uncertain as to whether I should accept what he was doing. Every time he came, before he left, he would ask if he could come again! I couldn't say no, but I didn't feel enthusiastic about him returning. Then one day, the minister asked if he could bring his wife with him next time he visited. He used to come every Tuesday. I said, "If you want to bring your wife, bring your wife!" In Arabic culture it would have been rude to say no!

For seven months, they came every Tuesday to read the Bible to George and speak to him about Christ. Every time they came I felt my blood pressure going up and I felt sick! On the 25 and 26 December 1981 we celebrated Christmas and on the 27th my husband went to his olive grove to tend our trees. While there he was taken suddenly ill. Somebody found him and took him to hospital. He had suffered a severe heart attack. On hearing what had happened and expecting my husband to die, people started coming to our home because, in Arabic culture, if somebody dies, the home has to be cleaned. So these people started to arrive to clean our house.

At the same time, the minister who had been visiting us every Tuesday arrived not knowing that my husband had suffered a heart attack and was in hospital. He was shocked to find so many people cleaning our house and asked what was going on. When he heard that my husband was very ill, he suggested we go into a quiet room, kneel down and pray that God would heal him. At this point I lifted my hands to heaven and said, "I need you Lord." I prayed to the Lord and promised him that if my husband survived and came home from the hospital, I would open our home for the Lord to use, even though I knew our Catholic relatives would be against us. But I promised the Lord that we would open our home for groups to come here and invite the minister to come and teach us.

My husband did recover and for the next twelve years people came here every week and all our family were baptized in the name of the Lord.

Hanna took up the story.

I was very young when all this happened. But I remember as a child coming to the church, worshipping and hearing the Word of God. At the age of fifteen, I went to a conference with my sister's daughter. My father was not sure whether I should go because, at this time, he was uncertain that what his sister was doing in allowing the minister from Tur'an to start a church in his sister's house was quite right! But my sister reassured him that he had no need to worry! And so, I went to the conference and received Christ there. It was 1990.

Hanna's sister continued:

> During the 1990s, the ministry grew in the home and around seventy people were baptized here in this home and in 2000 we were officially recognized as a Baptist Church. We met here until 2008 and then we moved to another place.

Hanna explained that the minister from Tur'an died in 2002 and the work was continued by the husband of Wedad's daughter from 2002 until 2013 when Hanna took over as the pastor.

We left Wedad and Radee but not before they had served us tea and biscuits and fresh pieces of apple. Having heard the story of how the evangelical church in Eilaboun had started, we continued our tour of the village and walked uphill and downhill in the searing heat to see where the church had moved to. Hanna continued:

> It was a very difficult time for us because the neighbour was very hostile towards us. One time I was in the building when the neighbour came in and started to threaten me. The ministry was flourishing but the neighbour told me he didn't want me here and he began to break several things in the church. I remember going home with tears in my eyes, asking God what was going on. It became clear we had to return to my sister's home, to the place where the church started. And for two months we met there without knowing what would happen in the future. We asked the Lord to give us a new place where we would be safe. And, thank God, that after two months he showed us a new place.

> We still have challenges. In Arabic culture, having your own property is very important. Church for the people is a building also. A building provides accountability and credibility and shows you are in a safe place. We know God has called us and he will be faithful.

We continued on our journey around the village and eventually found ourselves on the outskirts of Eilaboun inside a new building set high up with a commanding view of the surrounding Arab villages in the Galilee.

> We prayed a lot that God would give us honour and favour in the eyes of the people. Then one day, quite by chance, we met the man who was living here and he agreed to prepare this place for us but he also asked a high rent which wasn't easy for us. But we are here and seventy to eighty people come every week. Situated on the top of the hill, we pray constantly for our town of Eilaboun and for the surrounding towns that we can see from here. We aim to show love to the people here and be a good testimony by the way we live our lives.
>
> We are praying that very soon we will have our own place. That would be a huge thing for us. We are a praying church. Next week we are having 24 hours of prayer to ask the Lord to provide us with the land to build our own property because people ask us, "Where is your home? Where is your building?" When we tell them we are renting, this is difficult for them to understand because of our culture.
>
> When God called me he put in my heart a love and concern for the Arab villages here in the north. It's not an easy work but we know that God is the God of the impossible and he will open the doors for us to proclaim the gospel in the Galilee area.

There was a verse in Arabic on the wall of the building. "What does it say?" I asked Hanna.

> "We preach that Christ was crucified" (1 Corinthians 1:23). This is the power of the gospel, Jesus was crucified but he rose again.

We then retraced our steps and went into the centre of old Eilaboun, through the narrow streets, to a square courtyard surrounded by old buildings. Hanna explained, "I told you about the people from this village who were killed in 1948. These are the names of the people here on this plaque. This statue is of a woman crying for her sons. And here we have a memorial and cemetery. In 1948, the Christian families in Eilaboun were told to leave. I don't want to talk about the political situation; but the families were told to leave. Some went to Lebanon for a few months. Others went elsewhere. When they returned, the village had been largely destroyed and they had to rebuild it. It was a difficult story because several people were killed. I think the people who returned were very brave to rebuild Eilaboun again."

And with that, we left. It was clear Hanna did not want to say more. I knew I had some research to do to find out what had happened to cause such sorrow and pain. Before we bring Hanna's story up to date, it is necessary to better understand what happened in Eilaboun in 1948.

Eilaboun, 1948

Well known as being a Christian village, on 30 October 1948, fourteen men from the village were shot dead by soldiers from the Israeli army and the villagers were forced to leave during Operation Hiram. Many of them made their way to Lebanon for safety, where they lived as refugees before returning to Eilaboun in 1949. Why were they killed?

It was all a dreadful mistake. Villages that were known to be Christian were usually left untroubled by the Israeli army. However, Eilaboun had been occupied by soldiers from the Arab Liberation Army and they had killed two Israeli soldiers on 12 September 1948 and carried their severed heads through the village in a procession which made it appear that the people of Eilaboun had been involved in these murders when in fact they had not.

Enraged and misinformed at what had happened, the Israeli army entered Eilaboun and ordered all the inhabitants to assemble in the village square. The 800 inhabitants were then taken to Maghar, apart from twelve young men who were made to stay behind and who were shot.

Some elderly villagers remained in Eilaboun and when the village priests protested and demanded the villagers be allowed to return, after an investigation, the Israeli government allowed the people to return.

But the memory of that atrocity lives on in the minds of many in Eilaboun and other Arab villages, not to mention Palestinians who today live in the West Bank; people whose families did not return to their historic villages. And it is this legacy that casts a long shadow and affects the thinking and emotions of so many people. These are the people Hanna and Lena are working amongst. So how do you overcome these memories and move people on from unforgiveness and bitterness, to a place of forgiveness and reconciliation?

I first heard about Hanna and Lena from another contact I have long known in Israel, a man who is half Jewish and half Arab and who has worked in Israel for many years bringing together Arab and Jewish pastors who desire fellowship with one another and who seek to understand what God is saying to them about what he wants to do in Israel in these days. Two or three times a year, this group of pastors meet together, usually in a desert location in southern Israel, to pray together, share their stories and situations, and to seek to understand and help each other. It was to one of these gatherings that Hanna was invited just a few years ago. And this, he told me, has changed his life and outlook. Now he feels accepted by his fellow Messianic Jewish pastors. They still have their political differences, but they have been prepared to put those to one side and come together in a spirit of forgiveness and reconciliation. I have met many of these people and heard their stories. And for all, the experience of being accepted by "the other" is healing and progressive. It is supernatural. It is purposeful and represents God's heart. One of the verses that inspires these meetings is from Ephesians 2:

> *For Christ himself has brought peace to us. He united Jews and Gentiles into one people when, in his own body on the cross, he broke down the wall of hostility that separated us. He did this by ending the system of law with its commandments and regulations. He made peace between Jews and Gentiles by creating in himself one new people from the two groups. Together as one body, Christ reconciled both groups to God by means of his death on the cross, and our hostility towards each other was put to death.*
> EPHESIANS 2:14-16

Hanna and Lena have four daughters. How do they find living in Israel with parents who are evangelical Arab Christians, a minority within a minority?

My day in Eilaboun ended back at Hanna and Lena's house where Lena served ice cream! It had been a very hot afternoon, in every sense of the word. Hanna had earlier told me that Heidi, their eldest daughter (aged fifteen) had recently attended a summer camp for teenage Messianic Jewish and Christian Israeli Arab and Palestinian believers. The aim of the camp was for them to meet, have fun together, and at the same time share their stories and forge new friendships that would defy the forces that divide the two peoples. To find out what happened, I spoke to Heidi.

Heidi's story

Heidi began by describing Eilaboun through her eyes:

> It's a small village of between 5,000 and 6,000 people. The people are Christian. It's beautiful. Everything is close to our home because the village is small. This summer I went on a music camp for believers where we went to practise

our instruments together and learn how to lead worship. I made a lot of friends – Messianic and Palestinian – it was great. It was a unique experience for me because it brought together people from different cultures, different backgrounds and people with different thinking. We prayed together and we could see how God is working in different ways through different people. The first day, when we first met, it felt weird because I didn't know anybody. The second and third days were better and, by the fourth day, it felt amazing because we had got to know each other and become friends – Messianic, Palestinian, and also other Israeli Arabs from the Galilee area. We had a wonderful time and felt God was uniting us as we prayed together and worshipped together. I now have a lot of Messianic friends on Instagram and Palestinian friends on Instagram and Facebook and we all keep in touch with each other.

I asked Heidi what sort of a difference she hoped such gatherings could make to life in Israel.

I think this movement is important because God wants to bring about a breakthrough and unite the nation and bring us together as one in Jesus Christ. Every two to three months there is a meeting in Jerusalem for all those who came to the camp, to gather and see each other again, and worship together.

Heidi mentioned how she and the other young believers that she met over the summer of 2018 believe God wants to bring about a breakthrough in the spiritual realm in Israel. In seeking to understand modern Israel from a biblical perspective, it would appear that politics will not hold these young believers back – nor those pastors, both Jewish and Arab/Palestinian, who meet together regularly in the desert to pray together and work towards a unity that hitherto has been unthinkable, perhaps even unattainable – a unity that is threatened every time there is another outbreak of war or tension in Gaza or between the West Bank and Israel.

To investigate further, we must now turn to evangelical Arab and Palestinian Christians, to hear their stories.

12

PALESTINIAN CHRISTIANS – FROM GAZA

The situation for Christians in Gaza has been getting steadily worse. Ten years ago, there were approximately 3,000 Christians living there. Today there are perhaps 1,000 and they are mostly Greek Orthodox. What has happened?

Rami Ayad was murdered for his faith in Gaza in 2007. The people responsible for his death were militant Islamists. I met his widow, Pauline, in Bethlehem.

Pauline Ayad's story

Pauline told me the story of what happened to Rami, how she left Gaza with her children, and how she is now rebuilding her life.

I was born and brought up in Gaza and raised in a Christian family. I have two sisters and a brother. We attended church every week. I finished my degree in IT and I worked with the Government in IT programming. I did my degree in Gaza at the university there. I met Rami in the Baptist church in Gaza and a love relationship started between us. So, in 2001, we got engaged. Rami was also born and raised in a Christian family and he has two brothers and four sisters. When we met he was working in a bank. Two and a half years after we married he left the bank and started working for the Bible Society in Gaza City.

I have two boys and a girl; George is fifteen years, Wisam thirteen years, and Sama twelve years. Rami was murdered on 7 October 2007. At Christmas 2008, I moved with the children to Bethlehem.

Rami used to work in the Bible Society book store. There were a lot of people who used to come to Rami and ask about Christianity and he would gladly share his faith – he was never afraid to share his faith. A month before he was killed, he had an argument with a sheik there. Rami told me how the sheik came and tried to persuade him to become a Muslim. Rami replied that he (the sheik) would never persuade him (Rami) to become a Muslim, but that he (Rami) would be able to persuade the sheik to become a Christian. Then, in a threatening, menacing way, the sheik told Rami how he would "persuade" Rami to become a Muslim. When Rami told me about this conversation I felt very scared, although Rami was not troubled. "What can they do to me?" Rami said. "The most they could do is kill me and then I'd be a martyr for Christ."

I now understand that God was preparing Rami to die and be a martyr. Rami would always say that people who sacrifice their lives for Christ are blessed.

Before his death we heard the news that three people were killed in Turkey because of their faith in Christ. While I was shocked at the cruel, painful way they were killed, Rami had a different point of view.

On 4 October, when Rami was on his way home, he had become aware of some people in a car who had been watching him all day. When Rami reached home, before he entered the house, he looked at the men driving the car to acknowledge that he knew they had been following him. There were three men in the car with long beards and they looked very scary. Rami did not want to share with anybody about that incident. He only told his manager at work. Later that week, on the Friday, he received a threatening message on his phone. On Saturday, he went to work as normal. At 4.30 p.m., when he was due to arrive back home, I called him. He told me he was going for a short visit and he would be back soon. I knew that there was no place he had to go to, so I was worried and called Rami's brother, who then phoned Rami. Rami told him that he was "with the people" and then we knew he had been kidnapped.

We were worried. We contacted the local police and Hamas, but they told us they knew nothing. At 6 p.m., Rami called me. I asked him, "Where are you?" He told me he was a long way away and would not be back for a long time. When he told me that he was coming back, I felt comforted. I never imagined he would be killed. No one was able to reach him after that – that was the last time I heard his voice. At 6 a.m. the next morning, Rami's brother called me to say the police had called him to say they had found Rami's body in an empty field. He was dead.

I was really shocked. I never thought something like this would happen and Rami would die.

I asked Pauline whether she knew who was responsible for Rami's death.

We told the police all we knew, but after a week they closed the file. A lawyer told us the reason he closed the file was because he was threatened by people who were high up in senior positions who told him to close the file.

On the day of the funeral, as we were going to bury Rami, we were driving along the road and on both sides of the road there were many people who shouted bad and mean words to us. I know that they were trying to disguise the truth of what had happened and blame Rami for causing an incident that resulted in his death. But even the police inspector knew that Rami had done nothing wrong and now, today in Gaza, nobody accuses Rami of having done anything wrong.

Pauline left Gaza soon after Rami's death and moved to Bethlehem. I asked her how she has managed to cope with what has happened.

> It wasn't easy. Rami was the main source of income for the family. I depended on him for everything – he was the strength in our family. After his death, I moved in with my family and drew strength from them. Moving to a different place with three children, even though Rami's family moved with me, still felt difficult. Suddenly, all the responsibility for the family rested on me.
>
> When I first came to Bethlehem, a lady came to help me with the children which was a great help from God. She was only able to help for a short while, and after that I tried to find somebody else, but I couldn't find anybody. I felt God was saying he wanted me to be responsible for the family rather than entrust the children to somebody else. So I tried to find somebody who could at least help me with cleaning the house but I couldn't find anyone even though I was willing to pay! I felt God always told me the same message that he didn't want me to have anybody else in the house – he wanted me to be with the children and raise the family without outside interference. It wasn't easy – it was very, very hard. But I know God was telling me he was shaping me to become a very strong woman for the future.
>
> I don't know how, but life carried on. It was hard at first, but it has become easier gradually. There was a lot of pressure, cleaning the house, buying the food, caring for the children, but God always reminded me that everything works together for good for the people who love the Lord. And God always told me that he would never allow me to be overwhelmed, but he would always give me the strength to manage every situation.
>
> We sold our house in Gaza and I bought a house here in Bethlehem and now we are getting used to it.

"Did you ever ask, 'Why has this happened to me?'"

Many times, especially, at the beginning. I would complain to God and ask, "Why is this happening?" I felt I always had a love relationship with God – every time I needed something, he always provided. Growing up, God gave me Rami. He was a good husband. I would ask God, "You always loved me, so why has this happened?" Immediately I was reminded of the verse that everything works together for good for those who love the Lord. I was very sad when that Bible verse came to my mind, because I would ask what good could come from the death of my husband. At least he could have waited until after I had given birth. (Pauline was expecting their third child when Rami was murdered.)

It was a big challenge but then later I understood why. I now understand the good that has come from Rami's death.

After Rami's death, while I was still in Gaza, a lot of the believers would come to me and say, "You are God's daughter, you have to forgive." Back then, I refused to do that. And what I felt was, "No one knows what I'm going through – it's easy for them to tell me to forgive but they don't understand what's going on." Some other people came to tell me, "Let your revenge be for those people to come and believe in Christ." But I would say to God that I hated the people who killed my husband so much that I didn't want them to become Christian and that if I met them, I was ready to kill them; I wanted them to die a painful death and go to hell for what they did. I rejected the idea of Rami's killers becoming Christians because then they would go to heaven and I didn't want that to happen.

On the death of Rami, George was two and a half years old. He was deeply in love with his father – they were deeply connected. After Rami's death, George went into shock and would keep asking, "Where is Dad?" Back then I would tell him his father was with Jesus in heaven. Then he would say, "Why can't we go there and bring him back?"

He couldn't understand that his dad had gone for ever and we couldn't go and bring him back. George's situation went from bad to worse and every time I saw my son's pain, the more hatred I had towards Rami's killers. One time, because it became so exhausting to keep explaining to George that his father had died, the only way I thought I could help him understand that his dad had gone and was not coming back was to take a baby chick and kill it. So George and I took the chick and I killed it and showed him that it was dead. Then we buried it in the ground and I explained to him that this was what death was.

After a while, I came back to the Lord and told him that I knew I was his daughter and that I had to forgive those killers – but I couldn't and I asked for his help. I wanted deep forgiveness in my heart so that when George asked me about his dad, I didn't want to feel that anger and hatred rising up again – rather I wanted to feel forgiveness towards those men.

It took me a whole year of praying this prayer for forgiveness every day. As I read my Bible, God started talking to me: there is a time to live and a time to die. And God told me that that moment was Rami's time for death.

Then suddenly God started showing me the incident and situation from a different point of view. Instead of angry men coming to kill Rami, he showed me that God used those people so Rami could be in heaven with him. Rami was kidnapped for ten hours and during those hours there was a big fight between God and the devil. The devil took control of the body, but God won the war by taking Rami's life without him denying his faith.

Then my feelings started changing and I started sometimes forgetting about those people who had killed Rami. I started to understand that this was forgiveness and I told the people around me that I forgive those people who killed Rami and I started praying for those people who had killed Rami that my only revenge for them was that they would come to know the Lord. I saw the good in the story of Rami of how a lot of people have changed as a result of this incident and I have seen how a lot of people have held more to their faith in God because of the story of Rami and his faith.

But I still had deep in my heart a little dark spot where I did not have full forgiveness towards those people who killed Rami. I found that out by whenever the anniversary of his death occurred, I still felt anger. Rami was killed during Ramadan. Every time Ramadan came, I felt tired and even though Muslims enjoy good food during this month, I could not enjoy it and could not share with my Muslim friends during this time. That was until the summer of 2012. We were at a conference at our church and that conference was being held during Ramadan and the theme of the conference was the "Real Forgiveness". That was the forgiveness I was asking for those people.

At the beginning of the conference, I didn't think too much about it – it was just another conference. At the very start of the conference, the preacher said, close your eyes and imagine the people you want to give that deep forgiveness to. I closed my eyes and asked the Lord who the people were that he wanted me to forgive and he told me, "The people who killed Rami." I didn't want to listen to God saying that because at that time I was feeling angry because it was towards the end of Ramadan, the time when Rami was killed.

The next day the preacher, was speaking about Islam and Muslims and how we need to share the gospel with them. I wasn't focusing too much on what he was saying because it was evening time and I'd been with the children all day and felt very tired. The preacher asked those who wanted to give their lives to help Muslims and work with them to step forward. It was then that I felt a voice encouraging me to go forward, but at the same time, I didn't want to because I was tired. There was a struggle going on inside me!

Anyway, I went forward because I wanted to see what would happen. As soon as I reached the front of the church I started crying and I felt God's presence very strongly. I felt ashamed of my uncaring attitude when his attitude was just the opposite – he cared for these people. The preacher didn't know that God had told me I had to forgive those people who killed Rami. Then the preacher called me forward and asked if he could pray for me to be baptized with a spirit of love.

The next day, the theme of the conference was "The Real Forgiveness" and the preacher started saying how we had to pray for those who had hurt us, killed those close to us, or had a bad influence on us. I started crying inconsolably and saw a video in my mind of all the events surrounding the death of Rami. The preacher said, "let them go" and I prayed to God and asked him to take away all the unforgiveness still in my life. Right after I prayed that prayer, I immediately felt I was a different person. I felt happy.

Before the conference, I had told God that I wanted to go deeper with him but there had been something blocking this from happening. I wanted to be able to talk with him just as I did before Rami's death. So when the conference was over and I went home, and after the forgiveness that I had released, I felt that closeness with God once again. And then I understood and realized I couldn't go deeper in my relationship with him because I still had so much unforgiveness in my life. I argued with the Lord and reminded him that they, Rami's killers, were the ones who had hurt me. But God reminded me that I still had to forgive them.

It was soon after this that God showed me he wanted me to work with widows. At first, I didn't know where to start or what to do. It all seemed very hard. But a year after Rami's death, a husband of one of my friends died. I went to talk with her and it all seemed so natural, even easy. I understood her pain. When I went to talk with her, I was able to share with her my story and situation, and we encouraged each other. But to start an actual ministry with widows seemed very hard. However, after the forgiveness I had experienced, God told me, "Now is the time to start this ministry".

At the beginning I went with Salwa, our pastor's wife, and we would visit widows and I would share with them my story. I thought, "Why don't we hold a meeting once a week when we can all come and talk together?" And we started meeting once a week and God showed me that we should study the stories of widows in the Bible, to look at their lives and study the Bible stories. We then started a series for new believers and I can see that a lot of those women are enjoying a strong relationship with the Lord and they love him so much.

At first, I was only working with Christian widows and at the beginning I only wanted to work with Christians. But after last summer's conference when the preacher had told the story of Jonah running away because he didn't want to go to speak to the people in Nineveh, at that moment I saw myself being like Jonah. I felt I didn't hate Muslims, but I didn't want to share the Lord with them because I was afraid of them. I realized this was a sin and I felt also the need for repentance. At the first opportunity I stood in front of the church and shared with the people and repented before the Lord for harbouring those feelings. Then God showed me that I couldn't just say I had forgiven them and stay at a distance, rather I had to go and be amongst them.

I understand now that was the "good" the Bible verse talked about: "And we know that God causes everything to work together for the good of those who love God and are called according to his purpose for them" (Romans 8:28).

And now, I'm meeting with those widows once a week.

Fardi's story

Fardi and his wife and daughter were, like Pauline, also born in Gaza. When I met him in 2019, he had been living in Bethlehem for the past twelve years. So why did he leave Gaza?

My early years with my family were very happy in Gaza – I studied at the university in Gaza and gained a BA in Business Administration. The university was Islamic; 99 per cent of the students were Muslim. Gaza is my country; I love it very much.

My parents were traditional Orthodox Christians but I accepted the Lord in a baptist church. When I was young we were safe in Gaza. We could go anywhere. We lived amongst Muslims and felt very safe.

But then things started to change. I don't like to speak about political things but many Muslim people started to become extremely religious. As Christians we were considered with increased suspicion and accused of being pro-America and pro-Israel. People didn't understand about Jesus but, at the same time, many were hungry to know more about him. We spoke to many people about Jesus.

"So life for Christians became dangerous?" I asked.

Yes, very dangerous. In 1948, there were 50,000 Christians in Gaza, but now there are less than 1,000. Most of the Christians have emigrated. It's very dangerous to tell people there about the truth.

"You had to leave Gaza twelve years ago when Rami, the manager of the Bible Society bookshop, was killed?"

Yes, my wife and I worked initially with Campus Crusade for nineteen years and later became partners with the Bible Society there. When Rami was murdered, we knew we had to leave Gaza and we came out in secret. On the day we left, at 6 a.m., I told my mother we were going to the West Bank and asked her whether she would come with us. She told me she wanted to stay but encouraged me to take my wife and daughter and leave. And until today, I have not been back to Gaza. My daughter was two years old when we left and she doesn't remember anything about life in Gaza.

"You've had to start again and rebuild your life in the West Bank. Has it been easy?"

It's been another big challenge in our life! Not easy of course. But we thank the Lord for the Immanuel Church here in Bethlehem. I was baptized here. They have become my family. We feel we are at home here. God has taught us that we sometimes have to leave everything to follow him. I try not to focus on where I am but rather to find out what God wants me to do; to speak with people, to build relationships with people. I know God is with me and he has prepared everything ahead of me.

Fardi told me carefully about the work he is doing in Bethlehem.

I work with Campus Crusade; I have been with them for nineteen years now. We disciple new Christians, visiting many in their homes. When we talk to people on the streets, we ask them for five minutes of their time so that we can explain about our faith because so many have a wrong perspective about the Christian faith, through school and society. It makes me nervous sometimes but we love our people and our country.

"You have a vision for the Palestinian people: you believe God is working here. What is your hope for them?"

Yes, our vision is to share in five minutes with every Muslim person our hope in Jesus Christ. We tell them God is love.

He doesn't hate you or want to punish you. He loves you but he hates your sin.

Pauline's and Fardi's stories are painful. They have both paid a high price for their faith in Jesus but it is clear they understand that they have found the truth and they are not going to deny that, despite the pressure being put on them. From their stories, we can begin to understand that being part of a minority among a radical majority is not easy and many have left the region for a quieter, safer and more prosperous life abroad. It is also clear that they choose their words very carefully and it is necessary to read between the lines.

In seeking to understand modern Israel from a biblical perspective, we therefore have to embrace all that God is doing in the region, and clearly he is moving powerfully among Israeli Arabs (those who live within Israel) and Palestinians (Arabs who live in the West Bank and Gaza).

Could it be that the challenge Pauline Ayad faced, of having to forgive those who murdered her husband, is one that we Christians living outside the region also have to address? Of course, the situation is different. But maybe we have to ask God to forgive us for ignoring what he has and is doing in Israel by only concentrating on what we are doing in our own "cabbage patch" and ask the question, "Are we interested in God's agenda for the world or are we choosing to only look at our own local agenda?"

Even for Christians who "love Israel", perhaps the challenge is to extend that "love" to the Israeli Arabs and Palestinians in the region. After all, God does not have favourites! He clearly has different "callings" for people – but is that different to having favourites and preferring one people over another?

We will explore further what it means to be an evangelical Christian living in the West Bank in the next chapter.

13

PALESTINIAN STORIES FROM THE WEST BANK

It is a fact of life in Israel today, that if you are a Palestinian living in the West Bank, you cannot ignore the political situation and the physical divide that keeps people apart – in this case "the security wall" that borders the West Bank with Israel. Entering the West Bank involves going through border control, showing your passport if you're a foreigner or your ID if you're a local. It is not a pleasant experience for anybody and can be frustrating and humiliating for Palestinians.

To keep our eye on the subject matter of this book, we have to be careful not to get stuck in the swamp of politics and injustice and consciously seek to understand modern Israel from a biblical perspective. Of course, that does not mean we turn a blind eye to injustice. Rather, it means we do not allow injustice to cloud our view of God but rather motivate us to see his heart and work with him on bringing his peace and his solution to people living in misery and poverty.

In Bethlehem today, the number of Christians has fallen from over 90 per cent to less than 10 per cent. The majority of people living there today are Muslims. In other areas of the West Bank, the people living in the towns and villages are 100 per cent Islamic, often radical Muslims. Of the 10 per cent of Christians living in the very town where Jesus was born, less than 1 per cent would describe themselves as evangelical, the remainder are either Catholic or Orthodox Christians (Greek or Syrian).

Rhema Halabi describes herself as an evangelical Christian. But it hasn't always been that way. I met Rhema in September 2019 and she agreed to share her story.

Rhema Halabi's story

This is the story of an Arab Christian who moved from being a nominal Christian (an Orthodox Christian) to becoming an evangelical Christian – one of a tiny percentage in the West Bank.

Rhema is manager of the Immanuel Christian Bookshop in Bethlehem. She was born in Bethlehem in 1955. Her family were "Christian"; she has three sisters and three brothers. She went to St Joseph's school in Bethlehem. She used to go to a Catholic church but, in her words, she "never knew the Lord Jesus". When she was still at school, Rhema's father had an accident and badly injured his hand which meant he was unable to work which resulted in Rhema having to leave school early in order to help support the family. She married and she and her husband have twin girls, another girl, and two boys. "Are they all still living in Bethlehem?" I asked.

One is in America. He's a Christian, an Orthodox Christian. During the Gulf War, my mother wanted to help so she used to take my children to her church so that I could have a rest. They would come home singing songs to the Lord. I was astonished. I had never heard such songs before. They certainly weren't like the songs we heard in the Catholic church. But I was happy to let them go.

During the Gulf War, we were warned about the dangers of poison gas so I covered all the windows in my home with plastic and made sure all the doors were well sealed. I was afraid for my children. Our home was small with one bedroom, a kitchen and a salon. It was all on one floor and I felt it was not healthy. So I sealed all the cracks and when the whistle sounded before a rocket attack, I poured water on the floor in case of a chemical attack and put the gas masks on my children.

One day, as I was helping my seven year-old-son with his mask, he told me he wanted to die. "I don't want to live like this in fear," he told me. We lived near Rachel's tomb (at the entrance to Bethlehem, close to the security wall) and there was a curfew every day which meant we couldn't go outside. The soldiers were close to my home. We couldn't move. We couldn't go out. The children had to stay indoors and be quiet. My son said, "I want to die because if I die I will go to heaven. But you will not."

I was shocked when he told me this. "I'm a Christian," I told him. "No, no, you're not a Christian," he replied. "You and my father are not Christians. You are only Christians by name."

I asked him, "So tell me what Christianity is?"

He said, "You have to believe in the Lord Jesus as your Saviour and you have to accept him in your life, then when you die you will go to heaven."

I told him that my mother had never told me this and here he was, a seven-year-old talking to me in this way! He said, "Yes, it is because you are killing me making me wear this gas mask and stopping me breathing!" I said, "OK, sit down. I want to hear what you have to say."

I called my other children and said, "Is he saying the right thing?" They said, "Yes, we were afraid to tell you because you are a very good mother, a very good wife, a very good person, you go to your church but you do not know the Lord Jesus."

And so they told me the story of salvation. I was very anxious and wanted to know more. When the curfew stopped and we were free to leave the house, I ran to my mother. I told her, "You never told me about this salvation." She said, "I am praying for you."

"Twelve years you have been praying for me," I replied, "and you never told me this! It's not good."

I had to run home again quickly as the curfew came back into force. "Turn on your radio," she told me, "and find Radio Monte Carlo. They are putting all the messages there."

I ran back home and my husband asked, "Where were you?"

"With my mother," I replied.

My son told me, "Now you have to take all the plastic away and open the doors and windows! Do not be afraid."

I agreed as I was very tired of living like this. We opened the doors and windows, and then the whistle – the alarm – sounded. Rockets were being fired. But as I stood looking out of the window I realized I was no longer afraid. But still I didn't know how to accept the Lord Jesus.

I didn't have a radio so I asked my husband if he could get one for me. He remembered his mother had one so I asked my mother-in-law if I could borrow it.

"Be careful," she told me. "Don't break it!"

A few days later, it fell onto the floor and fearing further damage, I gave it back to her and instead started reading a Bible.

But I was frequently tired from the curfews and shouting from the soldiers; we were living under constant pressure.

One day, soon after, my mother called me to say an Egyptian pastor was coming to speak at the Baptist Church and she asked me to come and listen. I was keen to go but the problem was we had been invited to an engagement party on that day and had only two hours of freedom when the curfew was lifted. I told my husband, "I want to go to the church and see what's going on."

I ran to the church and this huge man from Egypt was playing music and singing songs that seemed to be all about me; "I was lost and you found me." And then he began to preach. He preached about the five foolish bridesmaids and the five wise bridesmaids. I realized I was one of the foolish ones. I realized I had very little time as my husband was expecting me to go with him to the engagement party.

As I rushed back home, I realized time was not on my side and I prayed, "Please Lord, my husband is very nice; don't let him shout and ask me why I'm late!"

When I reached the house, my husband said, "Are you coming to your friend's house?" "Yes, I replied, I'm ready!" And then I prayed another prayer, "Please Lord, let this engagement party be late in starting!" And it happened: the bride and bridegroom were late in arriving!

And so it was; I continued reading the Bible and going to the church with my mother and children. I gave my life to the Lord Jesus and was baptized and filled with the Holy Spirit. It all happened so quickly. My husband came to the Lord one year after me. All this happened as a result of our seven-year-old son speaking to me.

"Here you are in the bookshop on Manger Street in Bethlehem. People are going up and down all the time. Bethlehem today is no longer a majority Christian city. Only 1 per cent of the people there today call themselves Christian and the majority of those are Orthodox Christians. Most of the people who live here are Muslims. Do they come into the shop? Are they interested in what you do here?" I asked Rhema.

People are tired in Bethlehem. We live behind the wall. There are not enough jobs. When we first opened the bookshop, the traditional churches opposed us because they thought we were Jehovah's Witnesses. We place free Bibles, leaflets, the Jesus video and CDs on a table on the street outside – most of them are about salvation – and people help themselves. Many people come into the shop and ask about our faith. We want to be a light here in Bethlehem.

14

WHAT IS A MESSIANIC JEW?

Having read the stories of a variety of people so far in this book, you may be wondering how this jigsaw puzzle of Israel fits together.

It is time to explore Israeli society and fully appreciate how complex it is and wonder what God is doing to bring all his plans to fruition. Many Christians believe the Bible would indicate we are living in "the last days" that the Old Testament prophets and Jesus frequently referred to. If that is the case, then why bring the Jews back to Israel into such a complex and troubled scenario? This chapter will consider some of the questions you may be asking and seek to provide answers.

In Israel today there are many Jews who were born in the land. They are called Sabras after a fruit that has prickles on the outside but inside is soft, sweet, and juicy! As we have already discovered, there are also millions of Jews who have made Aliyah – that is, come to live in Israel after centuries of living in other countries. The major reason for so many Jewish people coming to live in Israel in recent times is undoubtedly due to the rapid rise in anti-Semitism in Germany in the 1930s, followed by the Holocaust in Europe during the Second World War.

How many Jewish people are there in the world?

According to a recent report by the Jewish Agency, there are 14.8 million Jewish people in the world today.4 5.7 million live in the United States and 2.4 million in other nations of the world (not including Israel). Approximate figures show that France is currently home to 450,000 Jews, followed by Canada with 392,000, and then the UK with 263,000. There are also Jews living in Arab and Muslim countries – with 15,000 in Turkey, around 8,000 in Iran, 2,000 in Morocco and approximately 1,000 in Tunisia.

It is interesting to note the following statistics: in 1939, prior to the Second World War, there were 16.7 million Jewish people worldwide. In 1945, post-Holocaust, that number had dropped to 11 million. In 1948 the number had risen slightly to 11.5 million.

How many Jewish people live in Israel?

According to the Central Bureau of Statistics in Israel, in November 2019, out of a total population of 9.1 million people in Israel, 6.7 million were Jewish (74 per cent) and 1.9 million were Arab (21 per cent). Approximately 430,000 Jewish people live in the West Bank, accounting for 15 per cent of the population there.

---

4   Sergio Della Pergola, "World Jewish Population, 2019" in A. Dashefsky and I. Sheskin (eds), *American Jewish Year Book 2019*, vol 119, Springer, 2020. These figures only include those people who define themselves as Jews and do not identify with another religion.

What do Jewish people living in Israel believe?

Visit Jerusalem and you are met with an array of religious Orthodox Jews who, while easily recognizable by their dress, vary slightly as to the "denomination" of Judaism they belong to.

Visit the Western Wall or areas in Jerusalem where the ultra-Orthodox live and you could easily be persuaded that the majority of Jews are religious! However, recent findings show the following: 10 per cent describe themselves as ultra-Orthodox; 11 per cent as religious; 13 per cent as traditional-religious; 22 per cent as traditional, and 43 per cent as secular.

Perhaps the next question to ask is, what about Messianic Jews in Israel? How many are there? What is life like for them?

Victor Kalisher's story

Victor Kalisher has lived in Israel all his life and has watched Israeli society develop. When I first met him in November 2017, I asked him how he would describe himself. Here's what he said,

> I'm a Jewish follower of Christ or a "Messianic Jew" as some people like to call us, and the Director of the Bible Society in Israel.

Victor's father was a Holocaust survivor. He was born in Poland in 1928 and eventually arrived in Israel after the Second World War and before the War of Independence, in which he fought. His was a miraculous story of survival. He later met his wife (Victor's mother) and they became one of the first Messianic Jewish families in the country. Victor responded to my brief introduction to his story:

> Yes, that's all true and when you say it like that it sounds very nostalgic! But I can tell you that growing up as one

who is part of this strange group of people who believed in Jesus, back then, people did not look positively on you, to say the least. In those days, there were hardly any believers in the land so growing up I knew that we were not like anyone else; we were different. At a very young age, I remember our neighbours would throw stones at our windows; there was a lot of hostility back then.

"So you were physically attacked as a family because they, your Jewish neighbours, blamed Jesus for the Holocaust?" I asked.

Yes, I remember from a very young age, they would send their kids to beat us. I remember that after my wife and I married and we had young children, our neighbours would be afraid to send their children to play with our children because they were concerned we would influence them.

Today the situation is much better. I can look back and see how God has performed miracles because when I was growing up there were so few believers in the land. Then, there was a small Messianic congregation in Jerusalem; today there are at least forty congregations in Jerusalem and over 120 around the country with thousands of believers. That may not sound a lot compared to the size of our population. But it is a lot compared to what it was. When I was at school, I was the only believer. When I was in the Israeli Navy, I was the only believer there. Today in schools there are many believers and in the Israeli Defence Forces (IDF) there are hundreds and they meet together and they encourage each other and they pray for each other and they want to be a testimony to society. It was never like that before in Israel. The testimony of believers in Israeli society today has not been like it is now for 2,000 years. So this is something which is new and we are excited about it.

"The numbers of believers may have grown considerably since those early days, but, even so, the numbers are still quite low?" I suggested.

I think there are around 15,000 Messianic believers – it's a fraction of society, but we are recognized as a group within Jewish society.

As Victor has already mentioned, after 2,000 years, this is the first time there has been a large group of Jewish believers in the land. I asked him to describe what it was like for him as a child at the beginning of this new movement.

When I was young, I never had the perspective that I was part of a new movement. Later on, when I grew up, then definitely, yes. Then I realized the meaning of being a believer as a Jew. Gradually, as a child growing up I began to realize I was privileged to be one of very, very few that God had chosen to reveal the truth about the Messiah of Israel. It was only by the grace of God, but I was one of a few. As well, God had saved my father from the fire, from the Holocaust. And I felt God had saved him for me and for my brothers. So God did miracles, in my eyes, in saving my father and mother during such a dreadful time in human history so that I could be born into a believing family. I realized this was very special for me. But yet, I felt alone.

"Did you have a strong sense of destiny and understanding of the times?"

Yes I did, especially because of the teaching in our congregation. We were taught a lot about what it means to be a Jew who believes in Christ. People couldn't understand this: How could you as a Jew believe in Christ? Christianity was for the Gentiles, not for Jews. To Jewish people, believing in Christ was a total contradiction. I learned that for me, as a Jew, to believe in Christ was not a contradiction. On the contrary, as a Jew, it didn't contradict with my Jewish identity, it actually fulfilled it – it was complementary. People get confused between Judaism and being a Jew. Being a Jew is my ethnic belonging – it's not a religion for me. That's who I am! You're English. I'm a Jew! So I grew up realizing something very special was happening and God was starting something new. Reading the Bible we understood that one day, God was going to restore his people. He was going to do it gradually. He would bring them to the land and then he would fill them with his Holy Spirit. And in a sense we, the local believers of today, are the first fruits of what God is still going to do.

"You have described a growing movement. Twenty years ago, I detected believers were fearful. Today there seems much more boldness: is that true?"

Definitely so. When I was growing up you would think twice about who to share your faith with and how to share it. It felt like I had to apologize because immediately people would think, "Don't you know what happened?" When I told my Bible teacher at school that I believed in Yeshua Jesus, she looked at me and said, "Victor, don't you ever forget how much Jewish blood was shed through history." That's what people understood – the persecution and the relationship of Jews with the Christian world. My teacher couldn't understand how I could justify history.

Today it's totally different and, today, Jews who believe in Jesus realize and understand that he fulfilled the Jewish Messianic expectation. And today they feel much more comfortable and more confident because there are so many others who believe. A few thousand may not sound a lot, but it's a very small country and people do know about us now.

I'll give you an example – my daughter is at high school and she and her believing friends started a prayer meeting every week at school. This is a secular school. There were between twelve and fourteen believers there. They would come every Monday at 7 o'clock in the morning for a time of prayer before school started at 8 a.m. And the teachers knew! So, yes, they are far more confident today to share about their faith.

"You are now Director of Bible Society work in Jerusalem. What drew you to this work?"

The answer to that question began when I was a child. I knew then that God was calling me to ministry and that's because of a dream that I had and that dream stayed with me through the years. So I had the calling and the knowledge that God wanted me to serve him. As a child I didn't understand what that meant. But as I grew up, I began to understand more. I finished my studies at school and completed my military service, becoming a naval officer. I did six years military service before joining a high tech company where I worked for eighteen years and where I was quite successful. But then I felt it was time for change. With my wife, I was praying that God would show me where he wanted me to serve him. "If I know it is from you then I'm willing to do anything and go wherever you send me," I prayed. I asked God to show me that it had something to do with the dream because that was something that I knew – it had stayed with me all my life and had something to do with the Bible because in my dream I was handed a Bible.

One day I was walking down Jaffa Street here in Jerusalem, and I saw the Bible Society shop. I thought to myself, I've lived here all my life and never been inside the place! So, I went in and started talking to the lady working here. She asked who I was and then told me that when she first came to Israel she stayed with my parents for two weeks! She then told me, "Before you came in I was on my knees praying that God would send us a new director because for two years we have been looking for a new director since the former one passed away. I feel I should give you the application forms!" This was on a Friday. She gave me the forms. A week later, on the next Shabbat, both my brothers, without talking to each other, called me and said, "You know Victor, the Bible Society is looking for a new director and we feel it is really for you." They had no idea that I was looking for a change. From their point of view, I had a good job at a leading company and that's it!

I was telling my wife about this and she said, "Well we're praying and these things are happening, so the least you can do is apply!" We were praying for two specific things: firstly that God would show us the connection to the dream and the other was for another child because we were having some difficulty having children. My wife said, if that also happens then I'll know God wants you in the ministry because giving up a career in the company and having another child would not work otherwise.

Over the next year I was in contact with the Bible Society. We had a first meeting. Then a second meeting. Then a senior director from the Bible Society office in England called me to say, "I'm coming to see you on Sunday, so we'd like your final answer because we'd like to have you."

I didn't know what to do. Do I give up a good career? I said, "God, I need an answer about that dream!"

The Thursday before that Sunday meeting, the only person in the world who knew about that dream called me. He was actually in Holland. When I'd had the dream, I'd shared it with a close friend of the family who was with us at the time. He told it to his friend who was now on his way to Israel and asking to meet me.

When we met, he told me he had heard about the dream I'd had as a child and he asked whether I would like to share the full details with him. So I shared it with him and then he said that before coming to meet me, he wondered what he could say to me and God had brought to his mind the story in the Old Testament book of Kings about Elijah being fed by the ravens. He felt that God would take care of me. He said it felt strange to give me such a verse, but when I told him that my dream took place in a street called Elijah the Prophet Street, I felt God had answered my prayer in a miraculous way. The only person on earth who knew I'd had a dream, came to Israel a few days before the weekend when I had to give a final answer.

I had real peace. I told my boss that I was leaving. My wife got pregnant! We have a ten year-old-daughter today!

"Ten years here in the heart of Jerusalem in Jaffa Street, where your shop front is very open about what you do, why are you here?"

We're here because God is doing amazing things in these times amongst the people of Israel. The people are still coming to the land of Israel today. Israel is a democracy – and even a secular country – thereby providing the best environment to encourage the Jews to come today, because if it was not like this, I dare not think what it would take to bring back the Jews to Israel. So God is using that to bring them. They are coming in their thousands for many different reasons; usually negative reasons such as anti-Semitism or the recent war in the Ukraine.

At the same time, running in parallel, God is bringing more and more people to faith. The local body is growing and we are seeing people coming into our Bible Society centre here. Recently, a group of Jewish people came from France and a lady came to faith right here where we're sitting. God is definitely bringing the Jewish people to the land of Israel and for us this is a sign that what God has promised to do in bringing about a great time of repentance and spiritual restoration of the people he is doing. It is happening today!

People come in here from different walks of life. Each one has a different question. We always try to explain to them what we believe, and what we believe is the truth from the Word of God. When we are talking to religious Orthodox Jews, definitely the conversation will come round to who is the Messiah and whether Yeshua Jesus fulfils Messianic prophecies of the Bible. They ask, "Why do we need him?" They have a lot of questions. "How come that God allowed a man to be crucified?" they ask. They get their opinions from all kinds of rabbinical teaching and so we try to show them from the Word of God that faith in Christ is the most Jewish thing to do and is actually fulfilling the biblical expectation of the Messiah.

One day a lady came and shared how she was going through a lot of suffering because her kids were behaving terribly and she didn't know what to do; they were actually hurting each other. She asked whether I could help her. I told her, the only way I thought I could help was to pray with her in the name of the Messiah and I would like to read a chapter from the Bible with her. She agreed and I read Isaiah chapter 53 with her. When she read that chapter about Yeshua it spoke to her heart so much she said, "That's what I was looking for."

Another lady came in and asked if I could teach her about Isaiah 53. As I started reading from the Bible, she started crying and said, "Look what we have done, look what we have done. How come the rabbis don't see that?" I explained to her that the Holy Spirit was opening her eyes to see the truth. And she said, "Yes, I can see that he is the Messiah, I feel like a curtain has been removed from my eyes." Those were her words. She came to faith here. So things like this are happening. Maybe not every day. But they are happening."

From Victor's story we can understand that to be a Messianic Jewish believer living in Israel is to be in the minority – but a growing minority! He was brought up in a home where his parents were believers. But what about Jewish people who were religious Orthodox Jews, but later decided to believe in Jesus Yeshua – what does that entail?

In the following chapter we will explore further stories of believers in Jesus who have come from different backgrounds to further understand the complexity of life in Israel today and how what you believe is what defines you.

15

ISRAELI SOCIETY IS COMPLEX!

Everybody in Israel has a story to tell! That is the conclusion I have come to after countless visits to the country over the past twenty years to record the stories of believers who live there: Jewish, Israeli Arab and Palestinian people.

This book is about understanding modern Israel from a biblical perspective. As we have already considered, there are many Scriptures that refer to Israel being "born again" both physically and spiritually in the "last days". The physical "rebirth" has been – and is being – visibly demonstrated by the thousands of Jewish people who have returned to live in their ancient homeland. Signs of the "spiritual" rebirth that Victor Kalisher talked about in the previous chapter are also evident as we now look at the stories of two people I met recently.

The first is Simon (not his real name).

Simon's story

Simon was born in Russia and came to Israel when he was fifteen years old to join his father who was already living here. He told me his story:

> I was trying to understand what it means to be a Jew. I understood that Jews have a connection with the Torah and I started to find Judaism interesting and I became an Orthodox Jew. I was living in Jerusalem. I joined the IDF

and in 2006, a few weeks before the second Lebanon war, I was diagnosed with leukaemia.

When I came to Israel I had joined a yeshiva (an educational establishment where Orthodox Jews study the Torah under a rabbi) and felt sure that if I followed a religious lifestyle, God would care for me. I spent seven years living in an Orthodox community.

A few years later, after being diagnosed with leukaemia, I had an operation followed by chemotherapy and radiotherapy. I remember asking God: what is happening? I was trying to live a religious life but I had cancer. Why was God giving me so much trouble? I was depressed and didn't know whether I would survive the cancer and recover. I was using morphine and then started using other drugs. For four years, I was lost to drugs.

I heard about a centre that could help people like me who were dependant on drugs and alcohol. I wanted to change my life so I joined this programme which was run by Christians. Today, seven years later, I'm a believer and I'm sharing the gospel and trying to help people who are struggling with life."

"How difficult was it for you leaving the Orthodox community and the yeshiva?" I asked.

Yes, it was difficult. But I knew I had found Jesus – I believe it was through the Holy Spirit working in my heart. I started to read the New Testament and I understood that Jesus is the Messiah and my people need him. I also understood that everything my rabbi had told me about him was not the truth. The truth is he saved my life from the drugs; he has saved my life from death from cancer and today I'm in full-time ministry in my church. I'm a youth pastor and pastor of home groups. I'm married to the perfect wife! She's the best God can give me! I believe in the God who saved my life.

Addiction

Drug and alcohol addiction is a big problem in Israel. Maybe not so surprising given the stresses on people when they come to live in an unfamiliar culture where they have to learn the language, find a job, and learn to stand on their own two feet. Many people stumble and end up living on the streets of cities like Tel Aviv or Haifa. It is in these places that some find help and manage to recover. Roma is one of those people.

Roma's story

I first met him in Haifa a few years ago. He was living in a rehab centre in Haifa called The House of Victory, or Beit Nitzachon to call it by its Hebrew name. Recovery for him has been slow, but sure. And today he is happy to share his story.

I was born in Russia in 1981. My father is Jewish. My mum has German roots. I finished school in Russia during the time of the collapse of the former Soviet Union – it was a hard time. Eventually I decided to leave Russia and move to Germany to live with my aunt. She was my mum's sister. I came to Germany as a crazy young guy. I did bad stuff – stealing and smoking hash. And finally I found myself in jail in Germany for six months. The German government told me, "You're a good guy but we don't need you! You need to go back to Russia!" I went back to Russia, and as I've already mentioned, my father is Jewish which meant I could make repatriation to Israel.

So in 1998 I came to Israel. I joined a programme for young people who wanted to devote their lives to Israel. I was alone. I had left my parents. I had left my friends. I had left my relatives. I was alone in a foreign country. My heart was empty. I started using drugs to help me relax and it wasn't long before I was using heroin. I lived in a kibbutz for approximately one year and then moved onto the streets of Tel Aviv a homeless, hard addict, stealing money to buy drugs.

One day in 2003 I met a guy who told me about the programme at the House of Victory in Haifa (Beit Nitzachon). I had been living on the streets of Tel Aviv for two years. I entered the programme and for the first time in my life I heard about Jesus and what he did for me on the cross. But I didn't take it seriously. Then I was still trusting only in myself and after six months I left the programme and inevitably, the result was bad. I turned my back on Jesus and went back to taking drugs. For the next seven years, until 2010 I used drugs.

In 2010 I returned to the House of Victory. And again I left because I still thought I could manage on my own.

My father passed away in 2015. I was a terrible drug addict. One night, I heard clearly the voice of Jesus. He told me, "How long do you think you can play games with me? For how long can you reject me?" The next morning I took my bag, I left the apartment where I had been sleeping and I ran to the House of Victory. It was April 2017.

This time, I caught hold of Jesus and I held onto him. The times before in 2003 and 2010 when I had left, the reason was I hadn't dedicated myself completely to Jesus. I still had some dark corner in my heart that thought I could manage on my own. Today, I belong fully to Jesus!

Today I'm smiling because I'm free!

God has worked miracles in my life. I have paid my debts; I was full of debts. I saw my mum recently. I hadn't seen her for fifteen years. During the summer of 2019 I went to Russia to visit her; she is an old lady now. We cried together. God is continually working in my life; I feel it! He told me, "My plan is not your plan." I know he has an amazing plan for my life.

Today I meet people who I used to know on the streets. I show them my pictures from my past life, how I was a terrible drug addict. They cannot believe that the person speaking to them is the same as the guy in the picture! Today I encourage the guys coming into the House of Victory to be obedient to Jesus. I share my story with them and tell them their past life is over; now they can have a new life. I help them, encourage them, we pray together; whatever is needed I'm there to help them find the truth, find Jesus.

Does God have favourites?

Roma's story is one of many I could tell you – about people I have met who have had their lives miraculously transformed, healed, set free, and been given hope, purpose, and understanding about why they are in Israel.

And it is understanding why they find themselves in Israel that can come as a particular revelation, especially to Arabs! It is impossible to fully understand modern Israel and what God is doing there today and ignore the Israeli Arabs and Palestinian people who live there. How sad it is to hear Christians in the nations take sides and be either more Zionist than the Jews or take up the Palestinian cause more than the Palestinians! From what I have learned by listening and talking to believers over the years, both Jewish believers and Arab Christians, we surely have to embrace all who live in the "Holy Land" and understand that each has a part to play in God's plan of bringing salvation to all who live in the land.

We know from Paul's letter to the Romans that, "all Israel will be saved" (Romans 11:26). But does that mean God has favourites? Of course not. Did Jesus die for the Jews only? No, we know that is not true. He died for every human being who has ever lived or whoever has yet to live. We are considering what he is doing in Israel at this time because the Bible has so much to say about this matter! Surely this should help us to understand the urgency of sharing the gospel with as many people as we can whether they be Jew or Gentile. When in Israel, it is perhaps the case that believers there are expecting the return of Jesus at any time. They do not talk about this all the time, because they understand the time is short and so they are busy getting on with the business of evangelism.

Some of the most precious people I have met in Israel have been Israeli Arab Christians who have such a deep understanding of the Scriptures and understand clearly the times in which we live according to the Bible, that they are incredible evangelists to everybody they meet, including Muslims! I have spoken to Arab Christians who find it easier talking to Jews rather than Muslims.

It is time to meet Sam Kawaneh, an Arab Christian living in Jerusalem.

Sam Kawaneh's story

Sam told me he was "made in Jerusalem"!

I was born in Jerusalem. For the early part of my life, I lived with my family in a small Christian village in the West Bank, before moving back to live in Jerusalem after finishing High School.

My grandma, who was an evangelical Christian, opened her house for the ministry for thirty-five years in the village where we lived. There were Orthodox Christians living there including Greek Orthodox and Catholics so, because she was unusual in being an evangelical Christian, my grandma was not liked there.

When I moved back to Jerusalem, I came back to the Lord, studied theology and for the next eight years I worked with Campus Crusade for Christ. During that time, I married and before long I had a family to support! In order to support my family, it was necessary to leave Campus Crusade and for a time I worked in business. However, although working hard, I had no sense of peace.

But two and a half years ago, I had a dream. The Lord came to me and said in a voice that sounded so clear, just like we are talking now, "I, the Lord, have called you to demonstrate my righteousness. I will take you by the hand and guard you, and I will give you to my people Israel, as a symbol of my covenant with them. And you will be a light to guide the nations."

I woke up – it was 4 a.m. in the morning. I recognized the words from Isaiah 42:6. I immediately felt joy flood my heart and I said, "OK Lord, I'm going to step out of the boat and start to do what you're calling me to do." I knew he was calling me to reach out to Muslims and to teach them how to love their enemies, the Jews.

Before that, I had started to pray, "Lord, use me to reach the Jewish people." My background is Arab, but my roots are Jewish. For a long time I had believed in replacement theology, that teaches God's promises to Israel are no longer relevant, rather the church has replaced Israel in God's eyes. I came to realize that replacement theology was a lie and I started to pray for the Jewish people and asked God to use me to reach out to them. But now God was telling me to go back to the Arab people. He said, "Go to the Arab people and teach them how to love the Jewish people. When Jewish people see their love, they will discover their Jewish Messiah."

So simply what I'm doing in the streets is praying for Arab people and sharing the gospel with them. After almost three years, I now lead two home groups, one of them from a Catholic background with seven families and the other one is with believers from a Muslim background meeting in a former Imam's house; he came to the Lord and brought his son and two cousins and now we are reading the Bible and praying together.

And that's all going on here in Jerusalem and the neighbourhoods of Jerusalem.

"It's a remarkable story of how God changed your heart from somebody who was into replacement theology to be able to love the Jewish people – that's a brave move – but then to love Muslim people. How did you feel about that?" I asked Sam.[5]

> Well it's not easy, but it's easy with him. Because when he said, "Love your enemy," it's not just words; it takes time to love and it takes effort. It means leaving traditions and old ways of thinking behind, like issues of land. What it means to me is this: what God promises, he will do. And it's clear – he said he would give the land to Abraham and his descendants. He gave the same promise to Isaac and then to Jacob. So he said this land is for them. So who am I to come and say God changed his mind?
>
> Another way of looking at it is this. Suppose my dad offered to buy me a car then, one day, because I didn't obey him, he changed his mind and gave the car to my brother. What does that mean for me? It means that my father lied to me. If we have a Heavenly Father who lies to us, that's not our Father. Rather that is the devil. So from there I started to think there is something wrong because if God lies, then why should I follow him? May be he will lie to me. If God is not speaking the truth, then who am I believing?
>
> Since then, I started to pray and he started to reveal things to me from both the Old and New Testaments. For example, when Joseph took Mary and baby Jesus to Egypt, after some time had passed, an angel spoke to Joseph and told him to take his family back to the land of Israel. He didn't say the land of Palestine! It was never called the land of Palestine until the Romans changed the name against the Jewish people. Palestine is not mentioned as a nation in the Bible.
>
> And so, after I realized replacement theology was a lie, God started to use me.

---

5   Replacement theology, put simply, suggests the church has replaced Israel in God's purposes.

"As an Israeli Arab, you are unusual in that not many would share your heart for Israel and the Jewish people. When you started to talk to people in your own circle, how did they respond?"

> Well, some of them hated me! Some attacked me physically. Some stayed quiet. Some of them agreed with me. But here's the secret – it's all about relationship and love. When we speak within a good relationship and in love, the message is accepted. If I come across as aggressive, nobody will accept me. It takes time to build a relationship with a Muslim. It takes time for them to trust you. But in the end you will see the fruit.

Sam's story leads us to ask another question. Are Muslims turning to Jesus in Israel and the West Bank?

We will find the answer to that question in the next chapter.

16

MEETING A MUSLIM BACKGROUND BELIEVER

One of the questions I am frequently asked is, "Have you ever felt afraid travelling around Israel?" I can honestly say, during the past twenty years of visiting the country frequently, sometimes during times of heightened tension and often on my own, I have never felt afraid in Israel, even when travelling into Gaza, around the West Bank, or within Israel itself – by train, bus, on foot, or by taxi. That is, I did not feel fear until I was taken into an area within the West Bank to meet a former Muslim. But then the fear I felt was not for myself, rather it was for him. He was risking his life to come and meet us. Let me explain.

It is said that every person who lives within the borders of Israel (including the West Bank) has a story to tell. This tiny country, the size of Wales in the United Kingdom, is home to a diverse population. Yes, the majority are either Jewish or Arab. But within those two people groups are further subgroups which need to be properly understood.

Israeli Jews are either Sabra (born in Israel) or those who have made Aliyah (come to live in Israel from the four corners of the world). Arabs can be either Israeli Arabs, those who live within the borders of modern Israel, or those who call themselves Palestinians, who live in the West Bank or Gaza.

Religious identity is extremely strong in the region. Among Jews, it is easy to recognize those who are religious or Orthodox Jews by their dress. Israeli Arabs can be either Muslim or Christian. Among Christian Arabs, the majority would describe themselves as Catholic, Orthodox (Greek, Syrian or Coptic), or evangelical (and although this group is by far the smallest of the Christian groups, it is growing). As a generalization, for Muslims, Orthodox Jews, and Orthodox Christian Arabs, their religion is what gives them their cultural identity. In other words, they didn't choose their religion, rather they were born into it and have thereby inherited that cultural identity.

The problem occurs when you decide to step outside of your inherited identity and take on the identity or faith of one of the other groups. For example, for an Arab to move from being an Orthodox Christian to being an evangelical Christian is a step that is not taken lightly because it invariably causes tension within their family and community.

The same is true for Jewish people who turn from being religious Orthodox or traditional Jews to being believers in Yeshua Jesus. For them, the cost is enormous and I have heard many instances of people being rejected by their families to the point of being considered dead – cut off for ever from their family and disinherited. The anti-missionary group Yad L'Achim are well known for targeting Messianic Jews in an effort to persuade them to renounce their faith in Yeshua and return to Judaism.

But the point of this chapter is to feature the story of an emerging group of people living in the West Bank. Little is known about them because it is too dangerous for them to disclose what has happened to them. These are former Muslims who have turned their back on the religion they were born into and instead embraced the God of Israel and become believers in Jesus. They are known as Muslim Background Believers (MBBs). Over the past few years, stories about MBBs in the West Bank were beginning to emerge and I was keen to meet some of them face-to-face to hear their stories.

The opportunity came in 2017 when I was invited to travel with a companion who was familiar with the area and with the people into the West Bank to meet "A", a Muslim who had become a believer in Jesus. When driving in the West Bank you need to know where to go and where not to go! The area is zoned into three distinct areas. Area A is totally under Palestinian civil and military control. Area B is under Palestinian civil control but Israeli military control. Area C is totally under Israeli civil and military control and is where there are Israeli settlements. These zones were established in 1995 under the Oslo 2 Accord. No Jewish person is allowed to drive their car into an Area A – the consequences are too dangerous and people have been known to lose their lives. Equally, no Palestinian is allowed to enter a Zone C.

My friend had been on his phone before we set off, arranging our rendezvous with the man we were attempting to meet. I can't tell you who took me, where we set off from, or where we went – that would be too dangerous for all concerned. We journeyed by car to an area of "no man's land". As we drove, the zones were clearly marked and it felt a hostile place to be. There were Israeli soldiers at checkpoints and Palestinian military at other intersections, all fully armed and ready to jump into action. We passed lines of people waiting at bus stops – Palestinians who were bussed into Israel to work in the morning and returned later in the day. It was clear that the aim was to keep the two people groups apart. I have noticed how the level of security in the country has steadily increased over the past twenty years due to the unrest (intifadas) and suicide bombers entering Israeli towns from the West Bank. In addition, the number of Jewish "settlements" has increased, so has the security surrounding them.

To return to our journey, my contact was taking me to meet a former Muslim who had become a believer in Jesus. He was talking to him on the phone now. I had no idea where we were going to meet and could never have imagined what was about to happen.

"A" lives in a town that is entirely Islamic, fundamentally so. It is a region that no Jew is permitted to enter for fear of their life. It is a place where schools follow a rigid Islamic curriculum imposed by the Palestinian Authority. Children are taught to hate Jews and desire martyrdom, and forced to follow an ideology that is isolating, cruel, and destructive.

A few years ago, a Christian man drove his car into the town where "A" lives and hastily handed out a box of Bibles in Arabic. The Bibles were immediately grabbed by the crowd of men who gathered round his car curious to know what was being given away for free. Who was this man? I cannot tell you. But I can tell you that he left his mobile phone number in each Bible before hurriedly driving away before the crowd realized the books they were taking were Bibles – forbidden books.

The brother of "A" was one of the Palestinian Muslim men who grabbed a Bible that day. In the privacy of his home, he opened the book and could hardly believe what he was reading. The person of Jesus and his teaching had an immediate impact on him and he called my friend, the man who had given away the Bibles.

This man (the brother of "A") became an enthusiastic believer in Jesus and encouraged others to consider his teaching. However, the Palestinian Authority police soon heard about this and he was arrested, imprisoned and badly tortured. Undeterred, "A" (married with four children) became a believer in Jesus.

We were approaching a lay-by with some trees on the side of the road. The car slowed down. A man ran from the cover of the trees, jumped into the back of the car, and we sped off again. Concerned we had been noticed, my friend was wary of the car behind us. But the other car went down another road and we continued for a short way before turning into a wooded area surrounded by high hedges. Confident we were safe for a short while, my friend turned off the engine, prayed and asked "A" to share his story. He spoke to my friend in Hebrew (which I found interesting) and my friend translated his story into English.

The story of "A", a Muslim Background Believer

And as we listened to his story, this is what he described:

My brother became an evangelist. He told many people about Jesus before he was arrested. He gave me a Bible and, as I read it, I saw the truth of what Yeshua said. I knew my thinking was changing, my behaviour was changing. I knew I had found the way of truth. The Spirit of God spoke to me and showed me the way I should go.

Reading Revelation 22:16–17 changed my life. "The Spirit and the bride say, 'Come!' And let the one who hears say, 'Come!' Let the one who is thirsty come; and let the one who wishes take the free gift of the water of life." [NIV]

Islam is forced on us from birth. I didn't choose to be a Muslim but I did choose to become a believer in Yeshua. I like the difference… It's my choice to accept his invitation to "come" and believe in Yeshua.

I have been a believer in Jesus for three years now. Am I afraid? Yes, I am very much afraid about what will happen. I'm not afraid of dying because God is with me, but, at the same time, I am afraid of what will happen if things come out into the open. I feel very responsible for the group of people I shepherd to make sure they stay safe and stay alive. My brother is in Canada now – he was granted religious asylum. Now he is no longer here, I am in charge and I have only been a believer for three years. I feel the responsibility of looking after the people in my care to make sure they won't get hurt. It's part of my task. I'm not afraid for myself, but I am afraid for them. I believe the growth in the number of Muslims becoming believers will continue but we have to be careful about who we talk to and where to go in order to keep people safe.

There are many ex-Muslims in my group who became believers through a dream. One lady who has four children accepted Yeshua after having a dream when the Lord spoke to her reassuringly and said, "Don't be afraid, I will take care of you. Nothing will happen to your children."

I know there are now over 300 believers in our town. We meet secretly in very small groups. The majority do not know each other; we have to keep it that way because of security so that if something happens not everybody is affected or even aware.

My wife and I read the Bible together but at present it would be too dangerous to tell our younger children about Yeshua because they would not be able to keep it a secret and would put all our lives at risk.

My views towards Israel and the Jewish people changed when I became a believer. Now I pray for them.

It was time to go. My friend started the engine and we slowly emerged back onto the road, and driving slowly to ensure there were no cars following, we returned to the lay-by next to the trees. "A" jumped out and ran for cover. He had walked four kilometres to rendezvous with us that day. And now he was returning to where he had come from – he was currently living in hiding in the air conditioning ducts of a factory. Members of his community had become aware he was no longer attending the mosque regularly and he knew they suspected him. It was not safe for him to return home. It was only a matter of time before he was found out.

The story that "A" told us is typical of many MBBs that I have heard about. Having spoken to a number of Arab Christians who are working among Muslims both within Israel as well as in the West Bank, it is clear that life for MBBs is very difficult. Even so, many have been baptized. Sadly, some have paid the ultimate price as a result. But their numbers are growing. Perhaps it is only a matter of time before their influence is felt more widely.

17

WHAT IS GOD DOING IN ISRAEL TODAY?

So far we have considered the story of Israel from earliest times and followed the Children of Israel as they emerged from Egypt with Moses as their leader and entered the Promised Land. If only things had worked out differently and they hadn't been sent into exile in Babylon – the painful years there could have been avoided. However, just as God had promised through the prophets, he made it possible for the Israelites to return to their homeland seventy years later. They surely all hoped this would be forever and never again would they be exiled from their land. But, history reveals that didn't happen and, for a third time, the Jewish people were sent into exile in AD 70, this time the period was for much longer – 2,000 years.

After such a long time out of their land, it would perhaps be reasonable to conclude that was the end of the story for the Jewish people. After all, what other nation has returned to their original homeland after 2,000 years of exile? Dispersed around the world for centuries, many Jews assimilated into the cultures of the countries they called home. So how come Israel has been restored to being a nation once again and in such a short period of time, emerged as a powerful, influential, and successful player on the world stage?

In this book, we are seeking to understand modern Israel from a biblical point of view. Starting with the present, we will now turn our attention to the future, to explore the development of the body of believers in Jesus in Israel and the West Bank today and find out how they understand themselves in the context of their history and the Bible, and how they are increasingly becoming a united body in the land – Jew and Arab (Gentile) – despite the powerful political forces that seek to keep them apart.

One of the few cities in Israel where co-existence seems to be working successfully, where Jew and Arab live peacefully together, is Haifa. Situated in northern Israel on the Mediterranean coast, Haifa is a large port city on the slopes of the Carmel range of mountains. The old, downtown part of Haifa lies close to the sea, around the port. In more recent times, as the city developed and building increased, properties were built into the steep slopes of the mountainside, until today, they reach the ridge of the mountain. The view from the top is commanding and from there you can see into Lebanon.

There are several Messianic congregations and Arab churches in Haifa. Each has its own story to tell of how it came into being. We have already considered the story of an Ethiopian congregation in Chapter 5 where Solomon is the pastor.

For the purposes of this book, we will now take a deeper look at another congregation where Dani Sayag (whose story was told earlier) is the pastor. Called the Carmel Assembly or Kehilat HaCarmel in Hebrew, it is here that you can really experience what it is like worshipping God in a mixed Jewish–Arab congregation. Founded by David and Karen Davis and co-founded by Peter and Rita Tsukahira over thirty years ago, this congregation has always sought to be a living embodiment of the "one new man" that Paul spoke about in Ephesians, namely a merging of Jew and Gentile in the Body of Christ.

For Christ himself has brought peace to us. He united Jews and Gentiles into one people when, in his own body on the cross, he broke down the wall of hostility that separated us.
EPHESIANS 2:14

When talking to Dani in November 2019, I asked him to explain further what this verse means.

The "one new man" is the vision, and one of the pillars of our congregation, that Jew and Gentile are one in Messiah. For us here in the land, this becomes an expression of unity between Jews and Arabs. It's very challenging because the atmosphere here in Israel is frequently on the verge of war and fighting and it's easier sometimes to connect and identify with your own people. Hence Messianic Jews can have more feeling for Jewish people and the Arabs can feel more for the Palestinians – it's a challenge for us. But I would say, if you let the politics of this world enter the message of Yeshua, of Jesus, you will not experience true unity. As long as we keep politics out of our calling, God can create "one new man". Our calling for the Jews and for the Arabs is to reach out to our people with the gospel of Yeshua, the Messiah, and to disciple them.

Our calling is to be priests of the Lord. I always remember the calling of the Levites; God purposefully didn't give them an inheritance in this world. He said, "You are going to be among your people, you will serve them, you will teach them the Word, you will help them, but you do not have any inheritance." Today, the fighting between Jews and Arabs is over the land, and it just goes backwards and forwards, causing tensions and war. But for us as believers, Jews and Arabs, we need to understand we don't have an inheritance in this world. Our inheritance is in the Lord. As long as we focus ourselves on preaching the gospel, to the Jews and the Arabs, God will bless it. When I meet with Messianic Jews and Arab believers who understand that, the depth of unity between us is so much stronger because we have the same calling.

I would appeal to Christians around the world: don't take sides because with the Lord there is only one side! He loves the Arabs and he loves the Jewish people and he wants to reveal himself to them and we try to express that unity here.

One of the ways we do that in our congregation is through our worship team. Every Shabbat when we meet, we have Jews and Arabs together in the worship team.

We sing songs in Hebrew and we sing songs in Arabic. The people in the congregation are a mixture of Jews and Arabs and it's a wonderful expression of unity. I say to people, if you don't like it, you won't like it in heaven because in heaven you will spend eternity with people from many different nations!

"Does it take a long time to reach that point of unity?" I asked Dani. "Many Jewish people have long memories of what has happened to them throughout history, especially more recently in the Holocaust. And, similarly, many Arab people have deep grievances over losses they have suffered." Dani explained:

It can take time. Personally, when I came to faith in Yeshua, I didn't like Arab people. I actually hated them. I thought they wanted to kill us and drag us out of our land. But when I came to Yeshua, something happened in my heart and God gave me a supernatural love towards my brothers, the Arabs. It was something I couldn't do in my own strength. It was supernatural – God took the hatred and replaced it with love. I saw it also happening with Arab people who hated Jews and how God put love in their heart toward Jewish people.

Praying for the peace of Jerusalem is not just about praying about when there is a war in Israel; rather it's about praying that the peace of God and the love of God will enter the hearts of the Jewish people and the Arab people because when that happens then truly we can love one another and show the "one new man".

It was time to look to the future and ask why God has restored Israel in these days. I put it to Dani that something I had noticed recently was a sense of the importance of mission; I was hearing about Jewish and Arab believers (especially among young people) who have started to form mission teams and go out together, not just within Israel but also to other nations. Dani replied enthusiastically:

In recent years with the emigration of so many Muslim Arabs from countries like Syria and Iraq travelling to Europe to escape war in their own countries, I know of Jews and Arabs who have been going to Europe, finding these refugees and reaching out to them with the love of Yeshua, teaching them and making disciples. I also know about groups who are going to Africa. Even in our congregation, the youth group are planning a mission trip to go out and express God's love. And this is the calling of this nation, to go out and be a light to the nations.

"So is this an ancient prophecy that you are seeing coming about today?" I asked.

Oh yes, when it says, "the law will go out from Zion" that is exactly what it means; that God's Word will go from this country to the nations. (Isaiah 2:3 and Micah 4:2 [NIV])

Looking further ahead to the return of Jesus, I ventured to ask Dani whether this was something much talked about by people in his congregation.

The question of the end times is a blessing when you teach it in the right way and you pay attention on the right things. But also it can be a very dangerous thing if it becomes your main message and your main focus. We have seen, not just in our generation but before, how end times teaching can cause people to lose their focus on what they are supposed to be doing now. People can become so caught up in the end times, they get busy with this line of thinking, going to conferences, reading books about it, thinking Yeshua is coming now, and this is happening, and this one is the anti-Christ – when the harvest is now! And so, yes, we teach about the end times and we see those times coming closer and closer but we are also mindful of the words of Yeshua when he said:

And you will hear of wars and threats of wars, but don't panic. Yes, these things must take place, but the end won't follow immediately. Nation will go to war against nation, and kingdom against kingdom. There will be famines and earthquakes in many parts of the world. But all this is only the first of the birth pains, with more to come.

Then you will be arrested, persecuted, and killed. You will be hated all over the world because you are my followers. And many will turn away from me and betray and hate each other. And many false prophets will appear and will deceive many people. Sin will be rampant everywhere, and the love of many will grow cold."

MATTHEW 24:6–12

We see all these things are happening and indeed increasing, and while we are watching events unfold around the world, at the same time we are equipping our people to reach out with the gospel of Yeshua as we realize time is getting shorter.

"Jesus said he would return when the gospel has been preached around the whole world. Is there that sense that it is returning to Israel and going out again from here?" I asked Dani.

Yes, it does increasingly look as though the gospel has reached almost the whole world so the return of Yeshua sounds very close. But I think God is giving us time now, to use this time to reach out with the gospel. This is him showing his mercy, not only to the people of Israel but also to the people in the nations of the world and we as believers need to be focused on that. God is going to use this nation of Israel to reach out to the nations of the world.

I asked Dani for his understanding of what Jesus meant when talking about the fig tree, "Then he gave them this illustration: 'Notice the fig tree, or any other tree. When the leaves come out, you know without being told that summer is near. In the same way, when you see all these things taking place, you can know that the Kingdom of God is near.'" (Luke 21:29–31)

> For me, when you talk about the fig tree, it means Israel is blossoming like the fig tree. When people look at Israel, it's easy to focus on the negative side with the wars and the Palestinian conflict with Israel, but there is so much more to Israel. When you talk about and see the blossoming of this nation, it's amazing how such a tiny nation can impact the world. There are so many things that Israel is creating to be a blessing to the nations. And the spiritual restoration that we are starting to see here is amazing. For 2,000 years God has been moving in the nations, but in the last seventy-two years, and even before that, God set his eyes on this nation and he is restoring this nation. Not many people saw what God was going to do in this nation. When people read prophecies about Israel before Israel became a nation (in 1948) they couldn't have imagined what is happening here today. Some of them even came up with ideas to suggest "Israel" no longer meant the Jewish people, rather "Israel" was now the church because there was no Israel! "The Jewish people are scattered all over the world," they said! So, for the people living then, they couldn't understand the prophecies. But then, around the year 1800, preachers like Spurgeon preached from Ezekiel 37 about the dry bones, and taught how God was going to bring his people back to Israel and how it was going to be a physical restoration and also a spiritual restoration and the people of Israel will know their Messiah. Men like Spurgeon understood from Scripture that God would restore Israel as a nation once again.
>
> And then, in recent times, after Israel became a nation, suddenly these prophecies made sense! Oh, God is

bringing his people – we see it! God is going to pour out his Spirit – oh, there is a Messianic body in the land and it's growing.

So when you talk about the fig tree, this is an amazing prophecy that has and is being fulfilled.

Being a Jewish believer, Dani was clear in his understanding of the verse from Ephesians that talks about the "one new man". But what about Arab Christians? How many of them share a similar understanding and are prepared to put aside their political and theological differences, not to mention the emotional challenge of forgiving people for what they may have done to cause hurt and loss of land.

In the next chapter, we will explore this further when we hear from Anis and Nawal Barhoum, Israeli Arab Christians who live in northern Israel.

18

EXPLORING THE "ONE NEW MAN" FROM A CHRISTIAN ARAB PERSPECTIVE

In this chapter, we will be exploring the "one new man" – but this time from the perspective of Christian Israeli Arabs.

For Christ himself has brought peace to us. He united Jews and Gentiles into one people when, in his own body on the cross, he broke down the wall of hostility that separated us. He did this by ending the system of law with its commandments and regulations. He made peace between Jews and Gentiles by creating in himself one new people from the two groups. Together as one body, Christ reconciled both groups to God by means of his death on the cross, and our hostility towards each other was put to death.

He brought this Good News of peace to you Gentiles who were far away from him, and peace to the Jews who were near. Now all of us can come to the Father through the same Holy Spirit because of what Christ has done for us.

So now you Gentiles are no longer strangers and foreigners. You are citizens along with all of God's holy people. You are members of God's family. Together, we are his house, built on the foundation of the apostles and the prophets. And the cornerstone is Christ Jesus himself. We are carefully joined together in him, becoming a holy temple for the Lord.

Through him you Gentiles are also being made part of this dwelling where God lives by his Spirit.

EPHESIANS 2:14–22

Anis and Nawal Barhoum's story

Anis and Nawal Barhoum are Israeli Arab Christians, aged seventy-two and sixty-six respectively, and they live in northern Israel. Anis told me he "worked as a simple maintenance man then miraculously became responsible for workers in a factory that only took people who had finished their military service" – something which he, as an Arab, never went through. Nawal was a teacher for twenty-seven years. Thirty-seven years ago, following a problem in the family, they felt called by God to "move on" and serve him while, at the same time, continuing with their "day jobs". They opened their home and started a children's ministry.

This movement grew and The House of Light and King's Kids were born! The Barhoums believe that, "All, with no exception, need Jesus." "For everyone has sinned; we all fall short of God's glorious standard." Romans 3:23. They believe the Word of God and the Holy Spirit provide the solution to all problems. They shared the gospel with whoever the Lord sent their way including people from different ethnic groups, people struggling with addiction, and girls who were thrown out of their families because of bad behaviour. Gradually, the Lord led them to start a Family Ministry. They encouraged the development of leadership skills in the youth and adults that they discipled. They spent time counselling people and nowadays they regularly visit prisons and hold camps and conferences for prisoners' families, as well as year-round programmes, camps, and conferences for youth, children, and their families.

Sometimes, after a ministry is well established, there can be a tendency to assume success has come easily. And so, I was keen to meet Anis and Nawal to hear their full story from the beginning, realizing, because of their age, they had lived through some difficult times between Arabs and Jews in Israel since 1948.

The opportunity came in November 2019 and we met one evening in Haifa. Sitting outside on a veranda of our hotel, overlooking the port of Haifa, I started by asking Nawal to introduce herself.

> I'm a Christian Arab from Israel and I love the Lord. Identity is everything in Israel, where what you believe defines you.
>
> I gave him my life as a child when I attended the Baptist Church School and I'm still wondering how kind he is in using me. As I grew up, I tried to shape up my own life, thinking that as a believer I was taking the right steps, but I didn't succeed so well. He brought me back to seek his will in 1977 when some family problems started.

Turning to Anis, I asked him the same question: how would he like to introduce himself? He hadn't heard Nawal's reply as he was enjoying a cup of coffee and talking to my colleagues at the time.

> I'm an Arab Christian, an Israeli citizen.

There was no hesitation, his reply was immediate. It was clear I was talking to a couple who were completely confident in sharing who they were and I was left with the impression that they would have given the same answer to anybody who asked them. Anis continued:

> I thank the Lord, he found me. When Nawal and I got married in 1973, we lived for ten years in the old family home close to my mother and one of my brothers. In our Arab culture, it is usual for the son to bring his new wife to come and live close to his parents and even share the same house. My father, who was already with the Lord, had given each of his five sons a piece of land and I planned to

build us a home on my share. But my brother liked mine and wanted to add it to his own land. He told me I couldn't build there. This made me crazy and I argued with him. This led to us fighting for two years.

I started to drink alcohol, thinking it would help me forget the problem, but the problem was growing more and more. One day, I took the decision that I should start to build no matter what the results might be. And I did. I built a strong foundation, then the walls, and was about to put the roof on, when Nawal came to me and said she had a word from God, "We need to leave this land." This made me even more crazy! My brother was against my building the house and now my wife was telling me we should let go of the land. Oh Lord!! Where else can we go? "Leave your native country, your relatives, and your father's family, and go to the land that I will show you." (Genesis 12:1)

After a long period of suffering and hesitation, I accepted that if Nawal had a word from the Lord that we should move away, then we should move away. But where to? All doors for immigration to the USA and Canada closed in front of us, although we have family there!

I tried to buy a flat in Nazareth. It was in a building where my friend lived. So, one Saturday I arranged to meet him. "It's Saturday morning," he said. "We have plenty of time: let's have some drinks before I show you the flat." And we started to drink alcohol. We drank more and more. My head started to hurt and I asked myself, "What am I doing here?" I had enough! Let's go and see the flat!

At the same time, just as we were about to leave to see the flat, another man who I had never met before, a friend of my friend, came along. "Why are you going to see that flat?" He said, "It is too small for you. In your town, people build their own houses." "But I don't have land to build on," I replied. "Come," he replied, "I have some land for you in your town." I remonstrated with him that I had no money with which to buy land. "Well how were you planning to buy a flat?" he replied. I told him I planned to take a loan from the bank. His face shone with a smile and he said, "OK, I have sold you the land. You pay me once you get the loan. The land is yours from now on and tomorrow morning I will go with you to the official offices to register it in your name!"

Was I drunk or what? It sounded a strange, yet reasonable, arrangement and I went home to tell Nawal what had happened. "This is crazy!" she said, "I trusted you to buy a flat, and you buy land! How many years will it take for us to build a house?"

We pray for miracles and when we have one, we do not always believe it happened. Maybe that's because they do not happen in exactly the way we thought of!

I told her: this is the situation. The land is in a very beautiful area of our town. I want to take the offer and with God's help, we will find the money.

We both received double power from above and worked long hours for five years. Thus the new house was completed and we moved to live there five years later.

Nawal took up the story.

It was a child evangelism fellowship – that's how it started in 1983. I invited our neighbour's children to our home, and then children from our town, and before long the programme became very successful. One day, Anis came home and saw seventy-two children sitting on the carpet listening to a Bible story, singing and worshipping the Lord, then memorizing a scripture! That's when the Lord touched his heart and that was the day he promised the Lord that he would serve him with me. We called the programme, "The House of Light".

Anis admitted that, at first, he had not agreed to have the child evangelism programme in their "new, beautiful" home. But she had told him,

Look Anis, I love you, you are my husband, but I love Jesus more. You need to know that I have promised to give our house to the Lord who made it possible for us to own a house.

Anis admitted:

Those words spoke directly to my heart and that is what changed my mind. I realized from my own experience of growing up how important it was to help children and young people. And from that day in 1984, we haven't looked back; the work grew and developed. God started sending addicts my way, one at a time. I have never been a social worker or someone who has worked in the field of addiction but the Lord taught me how to swim in that big ocean.

Nawal went on:

That's the age they get lost, if children don't have somebody around to guide and teach them.

It was clear Nawal was talking about the difficulties young Arab children often face in understanding their place in Israeli society as she went on to explain:

In my life, my family experienced being thrown out of their home in Beit She'an and coming to live in Nazareth as refugees with all the difficulties associated with that.

Nawal was referring to events that happened in many Arab villages in northern Israel during the War of Independence in 1948 as described by Hanna Eid in Chapter 11. Nawal continued:

Our Christian faith helped us learn after that experience to love the person who caused the pain and refuse to stay victims. We came to understand that the Lord allows us to experience pain and troubles in our life so that we can then help others who go through the same difficulties. The Lord helped us through those times. That's why we feel we are called and chosen by the Lord to serve him, in the way he wants, not in the way we want. He surprises us in many ways that we could never have dreamed of and now we find ourselves doing things that at one time we would never have wanted to do! But he sent us.

Over the years, Anis and Nawal have worked with thousands of children. The work began with Arab children, but soon developed to include Jewish children too. Was it always their heart to work with Arab and Jewish children together, I asked. Nawal replied immediately:

Yes, as I told you, the Lord has taught us from our own experiences of loss and trouble, starting with the experience of my family being thrown out of their home and later the experience of Anis's brother wanting our land for himself, that we have to see God has a different plan for our lives; a better way.

I remember my grandfather reminding us all the time how important it is for us to understand and know we are in the Lord's plan. So, this taught me that difficult things happen to the chosen ones because God wants something else for and from them. He allowed the disciples to experience problems and persecution so that they could later go and spread the gospel to the whole world. That's what I can see has happened to us. We can look back on our past difficulties and feel privileged that the Lord walked with us. Actually, he was holding us all the time and that's what helped us survive.

Seventeen years later after being in our new house, using it for the Lord, Anis's nephews came to see us. They told us they wanted to pay us for the land that their father (Anis's brother) had taken from us. We were surprised! We were not expecting such a thing to happen.

Anis and I discussed the situation. We agreed it would be right to accept half of the land's price but we decided we would not use it for ourselves. We could have bought something special with that money, or extended our house like so many people do. We then talked to our children and told them what Anis and I thought was the right thing to do and they agreed that we should do whatever we felt God was saying.

We used that money to buy some land. It was a miracle! The land was near a brook. The Lord had shown Anis a dream of a big bird flying, then landing near a stream. Anis never shared nor even remembered that dream, thinking it was only a dream. That was until some years later when the day came and we bought the farming land. Sitting there near the brook, the Lord brought back that dream to Anis's mind. He jumped in awe. Only then he knew it was from the Lord. Nowadays we use that land for discipleship meetings for women and young people. Children and youth camps are held there. Arabs and Jews can meet together, have fun together, eat together and listen to each other's stories. We organize several such gatherings each year and we always talk about the love of Christ that brings us together as one, united in him.

At this point Anis was keen to take up the story. Here were a couple who had found a meaning to the struggles they had faced in life. And all within the context of understanding modern Israel from a biblical perspective. It is so easy for us, who do not live in Israel or the West Bank, to judge what goes on there. But when listening to the real-life stories of believers in Jesus who live there, the people who have to make sense of the reality on the ground in a way that brings down the walls of hatred and hostility and instead promotes love, forgiveness and understanding, then you gain an insight into the unexpected, mysterious ways God works.

It's important to understand that this is the time to bring the youth – Messianic and Arab – together, to understand each other before they go off to the army, university, or work. We feel we are all chosen by God to form a bridge, a strong one that will not fall under each heavy load that passes above it. No difficult circumstances in the country can pull us down. We stand steadfast in the face of life's storms. The stronger our unity in Christ is, the more unbreakable and unfailing is our love for bringing others into the kingdom. We all need repentance and forgiveness. The story of my family is an example. When we left the land that my father had offered to us and built our own house on the (new land), the first people we invited to come and share a meal with us were my mother, my brother, and his family, so that we could say sorry to each other, show Jesus' love especially to our children and set a good example of God's inner healing in us. And it's the same for our two peoples: we need to understand each other and be prepared to say sorry. Often misunderstandings have arisen between our peoples because they haven't had the time to talk and share with each other.

That is why Nawal and I believe this time now is important. The farming land is the Lord's precious gift to us. We can bring the youth together in nature, work together and plant trees together. Each year, those who come eat the fruit from the trees planted by the ones who came previously.

I tell the youth: your friends did the planting, someone else watered, and God is the one who grows the plants and trees – and now you're eating the fruit and planting new trees for the generations to come. That is a picture of what you need to be doing in the land of Israel. You plant a seed of God's Word and then wait. Don't get impatient and say the seed is not growing! Nurture good relationships, let the world see, and the Holy Spirit will help them believe that in Christ all things are possible for his glory and the good of his children.

We went to Jordan recently, with a group of Messianic and Arab youth. When the people there heard us talking Hebrew together in the middle of their city they were curious and wanted to know who we were. They couldn't believe we were a mixed group of Jewish and Arab believers in Jesus. I explained to them that what they were seeing was Jesus bringing us together.

This is true reconciliation when we can cross the "wall" between our communities without being afraid. The challenge is not to put it off until some other time.

Nawal continued:

He has broken down the wall of partition, the dividing wall of hostility. That's why we are one. Jesus has provided the way for us to be reconciled but we have to learn how to live this reconciliation. It's very easy to say we love each other when each one lives in his own town and in his own environment. But to live together is a challenge.

It was getting late and Anis and Nawal had to leave. Their story of losing land only to be given the means to buy another piece of land which they then used to plant an orchard of olive and fruit trees is a powerful picture. Who would have thought that a piece of land could be so healing? A place of refuge in times of stress! A place to pray and listen to the Lord. But when that land is in Israel and the people working to clear the land before planting the fruit trees are young Jewish believers and Israeli Arab Christians then the story takes on added significance. As Nawal concluded, "It's easy to say we love each other... but to live together is a challenge." Perhaps when they start eating the fruit together, then the challenge proves it is possible when what unites them is a common purpose.

We now have to consider that "common purpose" and start to draw our conclusions from all that has been said so far.

What is God doing in Israel today and where is it heading? What is the end of the story? And why should I care?

19

WHY SHOULD I CARE?

"Why visit Israel?" is a question I am often asked. It may be a question you are asking yourself! Perhaps the best way to find an answer to this question is to talk to somebody who you trust who has been there and can explain what it meant to them.

Ann Pawson is a good friend of mine. We have known each other for nearly forty years. For the past ten years, Ann has been one of the trustees of The Olive Tree Reconciliation Fund – a charity my husband, Norman, and I started and which you can read more about in Chapter 20.

Ann has travelled with me to Israel frequently and together we have met and interviewed hundreds of believers, Jews and Arabs, for The Olive Tree radio series, led many tours and travelled the length and breadth of the country visiting ancient biblical sites, as well as discovering modern Israel.

The following is Ann's personal account of how visiting Israel has enriched her understanding of the Bible, inspired her to design a major piece of art – and, perhaps most of all, given her a personal revelation about Jesus' return to the Mount of Olives and his re-entry into Jerusalem.

The Golden Gate by Ann Pawson

During my first trip to Israel with my husband Richard in 2008, I was inspired to create a mosaic that would take me seven years to complete. At first glance, some people think this is a mosaic of Bethlehem; the star is an image that often depicts the birth of Jesus in Christmas cards. However, it is a mosaic of the old

Jerusalem, an original mosaic in glass and stone by Ann Pawson.
You can see a colour version of this image here: www.olivetreefund.
org/mosaic-of-jerusalem-ann-pawson-tells-the-story

city of Jerusalem, with the Mount of Olives in the background, depicting the second coming of Christ. One of the sights that enthralled me then – and still does on each subsequent visit – is the view of the old city of Jerusalem and the Temple Mount from the Mount of Olives and the fact that Jesus would be returning to that same place one day.

He was taken up into a cloud while they were watching, and they could no longer see him. As they strained to see him rising into heaven, two white-robed men suddenly stood among them. "Men of Galilee," they said, "why are you standing here staring into heaven? Jesus has been taken from you into heaven, but some day he will return from heaven in the same way you saw him go!" Then the apostles returned to Jerusalem from the Mount of Olives, a distance of a kilometre.
ACTS 1:9–12

That summer, Julia and Norman invited me to become a trustee of the Olive Tree Reconciliation Fund. As a trustee, I started accompanying Julia on her recording trips and, as we walked through the city of Jerusalem from one appointment to another, she would point out the sites and talk about the story behind some of them. On one particular trip, I wanted to get a grasp of the lay of the land for the mosaic – where were certain biblical sites in relation to the old city of Jerusalem?

Julia and I walked through the narrow streets in the Muslim Quarter, pausing every couple of minutes to let tour groups, cars, and taxis pass by. We walked past St Anne's Church, within which are the ruins of the Pools of Bethsaida, passed through St Stephen's Gate, turned right, went up a few steps, through a green door, and suddenly the vista opened wide. We were standing in the Muslim cemetery, looking out at the Mount of Olives, the Garden of Gethsemane and, of course, a long line of tour buses waiting for their disgorged tourists to return.

I had been here before. On that first trip in 2008, Richard and I had stood in the same place and watched the Palm Sunday procession descend from the Mount of Olives. We had heard the crowd singing and shaking their tambourines long before we caught a glimpse of the people winding down the hill, praising and waving palm branches.

As we paused and took in the view, Julia pointed out where the various historical and biblical sites were: Absalom's tomb, Zechariah's tomb, the Garden of Gethsemane, the Church of Mary Magdalene with its gold onion domes, and Dominus Flavit, the possible site where Jesus wept over Jerusalem:

> "O Jerusalem, Jerusalem, the city that kills the prophets and stones God's messengers! How often I have wanted to gather your children together as a hen protects her chicks beneath her wings, but you wouldn't let me. And now, look, your house is abandoned and desolate. For I tell you this, you will never see me again until you say, 'Blessings on the one who comes in the name of the Lord!'"
>
> MATTHEW 23:37–39

Julia explained that when Jesus came for the Feasts, it was likely that he would have come down the Mount of Olives, across the Kidron Valley, and walked up through the eastern gate into the Temple courtyard. We can read about one such journey, Jesus' triumphal entry, in the Gospel of Luke. Jesus, riding on a donkey, and followed by a band of joyful and palm-waving disciples, came down the Mount of Olives, and up into the Temple area where he then drove out the traders.

> As he came to the towns of Bethphage and Bethany on the Mount of Olives, he sent two disciples ahead. "Go into that village over there," he told them. "As you enter it, you will see a young donkey tied there that no one has ever ridden. Untie it and bring it here. If anyone asks, 'Why are you untying that colt?' just say, 'The Lord needs it.'"
>
> So they went and found the colt, just as Jesus had said. And sure enough, as they were untying it, the owners asked them, "Why are you untying that colt?"

And the disciples simply replied, "The Lord needs it." So they brought the colt to Jesus and threw their garments over it for him to ride on.

As he rode along, the crowds spread out their garments on the road ahead of him. When he reached the place where the road started down the Mount of Olives, all of his followers began to shout and sing as they walked along, praising God for all the wonderful miracles they had seen.

"Blessings on the King who comes in the name of the Lord! Peace in heaven, and glory in highest heaven!"

But some of the Pharisees among the crowd said, "Teacher, rebuke your followers for saying things like that!"

He replied, "If they kept quiet, the stones along the road would burst into cheers!"

But as he came closer to Jerusalem and saw the city ahead, he began to weep. "How I wish today that you of all people would understand the way to peace. But now it is too late, and peace is hidden from your eyes. Before long your enemies will build ramparts against your walls and encircle you and close in on you from every side. They will crush you into the ground, and your children with you. Your enemies will not leave a single stone in place, because you did not recognize it when God visited you.

Then Jesus entered the Temple and began to drive out the people selling animals for sacrifices. He said to them, "The Scriptures declare, 'My Temple will be a house of prayer,' but you have turned it into a den of thieves."

LUKE 19:29–46

This gate, called the Golden Gate, was walled up by the Ottomans in the 1530s and a Muslim cemetery was placed in front of it. Many believe this was done to prevent the Jewish Messiah from entering the city.

> *Then the man brought me back to the east gateway in the outer wall of the Temple area, but it was closed. And the Lord said to me, "This gate must remain closed; it will never again be opened. No one will ever open it and pass through, for the Lord, the God of Israel, has entered here. Therefore, it must always remain shut.*

EZEKIEL 44:1–2

As we stood in front of the sealed gate, surrounded by Muslim graves, looking out onto the Kidron Valley and up into The Mount of Olives, we spoke about the day the Messiah will come back with all the saints, walk down the Mount of Olives, across the cemetery, through those gates and into the Temple forecourt. As we paused and reflected on this, my eyes were drawn to the narrow stony path coming up the hill towards us. I had a vivid picture of Jesus striding purposefully up that path just in front of us with a group of people behind him. We were lost in our own thoughts and pictures, cocooned in stillness and oblivious to all around us. After what seemed like several minutes, we looked at each other and knew that we had both in different ways had a spiritual revelation.

I often think about that day and the image of my Messiah striding up that path and walking through the gate to take possession of his city.

> *Then the man brought me to the gate facing east, and I saw the glory of the God of Israel coming from the east. His voice was like the roar of rushing waters, and the land was radiant with his glory. The vision I saw was like the vision I had seen when he came to destroy the city and like the*

visions I had seen by the River Kebar, and I fell face down. The glory of the Lord entered the temple through the gate facing east. Then the Spirit lifted me up and brought me into the inner court, and the glory of the Lord filled the temple.

EZEKIEL 43:1–5, NIV

Visiting Israel

Ann's account vividly demonstrates how visiting Israel can bring the Bible alive! And there are so many other places I could mention. For example, Joppa (or Jaffa), the port where Jonah sailed from, only to be swallowed by a whale because he should have been travelling to Nineveh instead! Joppa is also the place where Peter was staying with Simon the Tanner when he received a visit from some soldiers who had been sent by their commander Cornelius who lived in Caesarea, requesting that Peter visit him. Caesarea lies further up the coast and this is where the Romans built a large port and Herod had a magnificent palace; you can still visit the Roman amphitheatre there. Here you can sit and read the stories of Peter's visit to Cornelius, who became the first Gentile convert, Paul's missionary journeys that began here, his later imprisonment before he set sail for Rome, and Philip who lived here with his daughters who were all prophetesses.

The Sea of Galilee is another place where you can sit and read about the life and work of Jesus: his calling of the disciples, their times around the lake side, the storm, the feeding of the 5,000 and the 4,000, the healings, preaching in the synagogue in Capernaum – all there for you to see.

And, of course, Jerusalem. A city that today is the religious capital of Israel for Jews, Muslims, and Christians. A place alive with spirituality. Sometimes it can be hard to penetrate the years of religious tradition that have almost suffocated so many sites. But, even so, its very situation, the Temple Mount, the Old City of David, Hezekiah's Tunnel, the southern Temple Steps – the very steps Jesus would have used to enter the Temple, the steps where Peter and John healed the beggar and thousands were added to the numbers of believers that day…

> Peter and John went to the Temple one afternoon to take part in the three o'clock prayer service. As they approached the Temple, a man lame from birth was being carried in. Each day he was put beside the Temple gate, the one called the Beautiful Gate, so he could beg from the people going into the Temple. When he saw Peter and John about to enter, he asked them for some money.
>
> Peter and John looked at him intently, and Peter said, "Look at us!" The lame man looked at them eagerly, expecting some money. But Peter said, "I don't have any silver or gold for you. But I'll give you what I have. In the name of Jesus Christ the Nazarene, get up and walk!"
>
> Then Peter took the lame man by the right hand and helped him up. And as he did, the man's feet and ankles were instantly healed and strengthened. He jumped up, stood on his feet, and began to walk! Then, walking, leaping, and praising God, he went into the Temple with them.
>
> All the people saw him walking and heard him praising God. When they realized he was the lame beggar they had seen so often at the Beautiful Gate, they were absolutely astounded! They all rushed out in amazement to Solomon's Colonnade, where the man was holding tightly to Peter and John.
>
> Peter saw his opportunity and addressed the crowd. "People of Israel," he said, "what is so surprising about this? And why stare at us as though we had made this man walk by our own power or godliness? For it is the God of Abraham, Isaac, and Jacob – the God of all our ancestors – who has brought glory to his servant Jesus by doing this. This is the same Jesus whom you handed over and rejected before Pilate,

despite Pilate's decision to release him. You rejected this holy, righteous one and instead demanded the release of a murderer. You killed the author of life, but God raised him from the dead. And we are witnesses of this fact!

"Through faith in the name of Jesus, this man was healed – and you know how crippled he was before. Faith in Jesus' name has healed him before your very eyes.

"Friends, I realize that what you and your leaders did to Jesus was done in ignorance. But God was fulfilling what all the prophets had foretold about the Messiah – that he must suffer these things. Now repent of your sins and turn to God, so that your sins may be wiped away. Then times of refreshment will come from the presence of the Lord, and he will again send you Jesus, your appointed Messiah. For he must remain in heaven until the time for the final restoration of all things, as God promised long ago through his holy prophets. Moses said, 'The Lord your God will raise up for you a Prophet like me from among your own people. Listen carefully to everything he tells you.' Then Moses said, 'Anyone who will not listen to that Prophet will be completely cut off from God's people.'

"Starting with Samuel, every prophet spoke about what is happening today. You are the children of those prophets, and you are included in the covenant God promised to your ancestors. For God said to Abraham, 'Through your descendants all the families on earth will be blessed.' When God raised up his servant, Jesus, he sent him first to you people of Israel, to bless you by turning each of you back from your sinful ways."

While Peter and John were speaking to the people, they were confronted by the priests, the captain of the Temple guard, and some of the Sadducees. These leaders were very disturbed that Peter and John were teaching the people that through Jesus there is a resurrection of the dead. They arrested them and, since it was already evening, put them in jail until morning. But many of the people who heard their message believed it, so the number of men who believed now totalled about 5,000.

ACTS 3:1 – 4:4

Reading the biblical accounts of what happened in situ suddenly brings the Bible from black and white into colour! To experience the story of Israel and God's dealings with the Jewish people through the centuries to the present day in the land where it all happened is, quite literally, to walk in the footsteps of the prophets and in the footsteps of Jesus. Israel is where the story of God revealing himself to mankind began and I believe the Bible tells us Jerusalem is the city where world history will end when Jesus returns.

Understanding modern Israel in a biblical context is therefore to understand where we are in God's timeframe. It is his way of helping us to put our lives in context. We do not live in a bubble! We are part of history – his story.

Should I care? The story of Israel should help us to understand God better and understand how much he loves every human being who has ever lived and who is yet to live.

There is still more of his story to be revealed. But the story so far should help us to understand the future that is yet to happen.

20

THE OLIVE TREE RECONCILIATION FUND

There are some things in life that we look back on and wonder, "How ever did that happen?"! The Olive Tree Reconciliation Fund is one such occurrence. The old adage that one thing leads to another is certainly true. I could never have imagined starting a charity, but that is what happened in 2008 as a direct result of people sending gifts of money to pass on to the Jewish and Arab believers living in Israel and the Palestinian Areas that they had been reading about in books or articles I have written, or in radio programmes they had heard.

In the beginning

It all started with an article about the plight of Arab Christians in Bethlehem – in particular those belonging to the evangelical community there.[6] For those of you who are passionate about supporting Israel, this article posed a challenge: can we feed first and talk theology afterwards? As I wrote then, "I am not saying that theology does not matter. Of course it does. Those who disagree with replacement theology (as I most certainly do) will never change the situation in Bethlehem by taking a stand-offish attitude. We have to go there, whether in prayer or in person, and get our hands dirty and help the people – otherwise, there will soon be no Christian Arabs left in Bethlehem." The

6   Julia Fisher, "Remember Bethlehem – a place of birth and sacrifice", *Sword Magazine, Jan/Feb 2007.*

article went on to describe the heartache experienced by one evangelical pastor in particular, and the sacrificial way in which he helped the people there, both Christians and Muslims.

The response to that article was overwhelming – and every penny donated was sent to the pastor in Bethlehem for him to give to those in need. It demonstrated that Christians in the UK, who love Israel and the Jewish people, also love and support the Arab Christians and recognize the work of reconciliation that is going on between Arab Christians and Messianic Jewish believers in the Holy Land today.

But why start a charity?

Over a relatively short period of time, more and more people responded by sending gifts and it was clear we had to act responsibly and handle this money with integrity. The aim of the OTRF has always been to tell the stories of what God is doing in Israel and the West Bank (and the wider Middle East) among Jewish, Israeli Arab, and Palestinian believers, especially those whose heart's desire is to see reconciliation between the people groups and unity in the Body of Christ.

From the start, due to the generosity of one particular person, we have broadcast a weekly radio programme across the UK called The Olive Tree. Visit our website today and you can hear the entire series – over 500 programmes to date; believers in Jesus from "both sides", from all walks of life, all telling their own unique story. Put these stories together and you have a tapestry, a picture, of what God is doing in Israel today. It is amazing, looking back, to see just how much has changed in such a short time.

This book has attempted to outline, in simple terms, what we can be sure of – God is quietly and mysteriously working out his plans for the people of this world before Jesus returns. And who is Jesus returning for? His bride. And his bride will be a church that consists of Jewish and non-Jewish (Gentile) believers. And the focus of all this activity will be Israel!

The mandate of the OTRF remains unchanged: we will continue to tell these stories for as long as we can, so that Christians around the world can better understand and take an active interest in what God is doing in Israel today – his story, which, after all, is the making of history.

How to get in touch

The OTRF is a registered charity (Number 1125706) which aims to build bridges of understanding and support, in a spirit of reconciliation between believers (both Jewish and Arab), in Israel and the wider Middle East with Christians worldwide. Our chief means of doing this is through gathering and thoroughly researching the stories of believers who live there, then broadcasting or publishing them in order to inform Christians in the nations who are interested.

That many Christians respond to these stories by giving generously enables the OTRF to pass on every penny we receive to those in need; and the needs are great and constantly increasing.

When the focus of much of the world's media is centred on Jerusalem and what happens there in the political realm, should it not be an important area of focus for the Christians to enquire as to what God is doing there today and look at the region through the lens of the Bible and the spiritual realm?

Information

For more information about the OTRF and to hear The Olive Tree radio programmes, please visit our website, www.olivetreefund.org.